More Reigns in Royal Robes

Exploring the lives of more Old Testament kings and the times in which they lived

Dr A. J. Monty White

DayOne

© Day One Publications 2023

ISBN 978-1-84625-745-2

British Library Cataloguing in Publication Data available
Published by Day One Publications
Ryelands Road, Leominster, HR6 8NZ
Telephone 01568 613 740 FAX 01568 611 473
email—sales@dayone.co.uk
web site—www.dayone.co.uk

Cover design by Kathryn Chedgzoy
Printed by 4edge

For
Rebekah
and Jonathan Paul

Endorsements

In this book, Monty takes us on a beautiful historical journey, giving us insight into the lives of each of these Royal Rogues. Such detail and acumen allow the reader to experience the Bible text in detail, cross referenced with Monty's personal thoughts and nuggets of wisdom.

Monty is able to intertwine the lives of each of the kings, showing you, the reader, how the stories overlap and cross reference with helpful diagrams. With a simple layout and quirky titles—this makes it an interesting read. He has brought the threads together into some neat conclusions which I find so helpful.

For those of you who enjoy the details of the Text, this is a book to add to your study time, giving context and history. I personally enjoyed how Monty brought his years of wisdom and obvious study, revealing insight, which is applicable to our lives today and, if we take note, will help us with the journeys and battles we face as people.

Rev Heath van Staden, Pastor of Liberty Church, Llanwern, South Wales

I met and married Monty's sister, Jane, in the mid-70s, when we both became Christians. I soon started reading Monty's publications and was very much inspired and encouraged by the biblical stand that he took in his books.

Recently, I found reading Rogues in Royal Robes *was a very different yet no less inspiring and encouraging read! Full of in-depth insights into the kings of the Bible and many great life-lesson take-aways! Monty's latest work* More Rogues in Royal Robes *digs a bit deeper into the lives of the Biblical record of leaders, their lives, loves and losses. The Bible says, 'there is nothing new under the sun' (Ecclesiastes 1:9), and this means that we can learn something from the Biblical record to help us now in these modern times—times where Biblical leadership, especially on a national level, is in short supply! I like that Monty always points to King Jesus and, at the end of the book, he shows us that all kings and leaders are just feint reflections of the King of kings and the Lord of lords—the all-sufficient One!*

I can highly recommend this latest book.

Pastor Stephen Harmes, Senior Leader of the River Dee Community Church, Flint, North Wales

Contents

About the author

Dr A J Monty White was converted to Christianity from atheism in 1964 when he was an undergraduate student at, what was then, the University College of Wales, Aberystwyth—now Aberystwyth University. One of the reasons that Monty started to take the Bible seriously was the fact that he became convinced that the historical events recorded in the Old Testament actually took place—many being corroborated by Assyrian and Babylonian records that archaeologists had discovered. This knowledge turned him from being an atheist to one who believed that there was a God and that the Bible could be trusted. One night, in February 1964, Monty heard the gospel message and, as a result, he turned to the Lord Jesus Christ for salvation through his death on Calvary's cross. His life has never been the same since!

Monty has written a number of books, booklets and pamphlets dealing with the subject of creation and evolution. He has also contributed chapters on creation in other books and has had dozens of articles about creation and evolution published in magazines and journals world-wide. His writings have been translated into Dutch, French, German, Portuguese, Russian and Swedish. Monty has spoken and lectured extensively not only in the UK, but also in many European countries as well as in Hong Kong and in the USA. From 1983 until 2001, Monty was a guest lecturer on the subject of the Bible and Science at the State Independent Theological University of Basel, Switzerland.

Monty is a graduate of the University of Wales, obtaining his BSc in 1967 and being awarded a PhD in 1970 for his research in the field of Gas Kinetics. After a further two years of chemical research at Aberystwyth, Monty moved to Cardiff where he held a number of senior administrative posts at Cardiff University until September 2000 when he became the Chief Executive of *Answers in Genesis (UK/Europe)*, a post which he held until July 2008. Monty then returned to South Wales and had an itinerant ministry speaking and preaching until his wife, Irene, took ill with cancer, when Monty had to curtail his ministry in order to care for her. Irene finally went to be with the Lord in March 2018.

After leaving *Answers in Genesis (UK/Europe)*, Monty developed a number of talks about the history that is found in the Bible and how much of that history has been corroborated by archaeological discoveries that have been made in the Middle East. Monty's first book dealing with biblical history and the corroborative archaeological findings that show how, in matters pertaining to history, the Bible can be trusted, was published in 2020. It was entitled *Rogues in Royal Robes* and it focused on the lives of some of the kings of the Northern Kingdom of Israel, although the lives of some of the kings of the Southern Kingdom of Judah were not neglected. In this present book, Monty looks in more detail at the lives of King David and his son, King Solomon, and the lives of some of the kings of the Southern Kingdom of Judah, from the time of the civil war in Israel to the time when the inhabitants of the Southern Kingdom of Judah were taken into captivity to Babylon.

Preface

I trust that the reader will not mind my being a little personal in sharing that I am in my late-seventies and people often ask me what I do with my time now that I am retired and my wife, Irene, has passed away. I often wonder what answer they expect me to give and when I tell them that I am interested in the kings that we read about in the Bible and that lived in Old Testament times, they look shocked. They look even more surprised when I tell them that I have already had one book published about these kings and am writing another. Invariably, they want to know more about what I have written and what I am writing about now. You would be surprised to hear of the conversations that I have had, with Christians and non-Christians alike, about the rogues in the Old Testament who lived in royal robes. Inevitably, questions are asked about how we know that these kings really existed and this invariably leads to questions about the accuracy of the Bible and then onto questions about whether God exists and how we can know Him.

I entitled the first book that I wrote about Old Testament history and some of the kings who lived at the time, *Rogues in Royal Robes*. I did so because these kings very often started out their lives as rogues and ended up living in palaces dressed in royal robes. As I pointed out in that book, one of the problems encountered by those who study the Old Testament and those who try to make sense of the history told in it, is the fact that no dates are given in the narratives and so we often find it difficult to follow the stories, especially if we are reading the life-story of a king in the book of Kings as well as in the book of Chronicles. In my previous book, and in this book, the dates given for the reigns of the kings of Israel—the Northern Kingdom of Israel and the Southern Kingdom of Judah— are those that have been determined by Professor Edwin Thiele in his book *The Mysterious Numbers of the Hebrew Kings* (New Revised edition, 1983, published by Kregel, Grand Rapids, MI 49501, USA) who, incredibly, is relatively unknown. I pointed out in my previous book that this is surprising, for this man achieved what no one else before him had—he established a detailed chronology from the data given in the Bible about the kings of the Northern Kingdom of Israel and the Southern Kingdom of Judah. This was no mean feat for, until Professor Thiele's achievement, no one could make the numbers given for the lengths of the reigns of the kings of the Northern Kingdom of Israel agree with those given for the reigns of the kings of the Southern Kingdom of Judah and *vice versa*. The chronology of the Hebrew kings formed part of Professor Thiele's doctoral programme at the University of Chicago and, until the publication of this research, the dates that were established from the Bible seemed to be at a variance compared to those established from historical sources of the countries surrounding the land of Israel at the time.

Basically, Professor Thiele accomplished two outstanding feats. Firstly, he established a single chronology for both the Northern Kingdom of Israel and the Southern Kingdom of Judah which got rid of all the apparent discrepancies that existed between the chronologies of these two kingdoms. And secondly, he locked this chronology into the established chronologies fixed by modern astronomical records of the surrounding countries, notably those of Assyria and Babylon. Professor Thiele's work finally put all the pieces of the chronological jigsaw together for the period covering the reigns of the kings of the Northern Kingdom of Israel and the Southern Kingdom of Judah.

My book, *Rogues in Royal Robes*, covers in detail the rise and fall of King Omri of the Northern Kingdom of Israel and his dynasty—this included his son, King Ahab and all of his descendants. The book also details the story of the rise of Jehu from his being an army commander in Israel's army to his being the king of the Northern Kingdom of Israel and his destruction of all of King Ahab's descendants. Furthermore, I detail how Athaliah became queen of the Southern Kingdom of Judah and how her grandson, Joash, was hidden by his aunt and eventually became the king. Although this story is about a king of the Southern Kingdom of Judah, most of the book is about the rogues who became the kings over the Northern Kingdom of Israel. This current book is mainly about the rogues who became the kings of the Southern Kingdom of Judah.

It is the usual practice to thank those who have helped and encouraged the author in his writing. I therefore wish to thank the following people for their help, while I wrote this book:

My dear friends, Carmen and Stefan in Ireland, who pray for me constantly, and Mike Grimshaw for proofreading the original manuscript—for his useful suggestions and comments and for his help in improving the grammar, sense and logic in so many parts of the book.

A big thank you to you all!

Finally, I have pleasure in dedicating this book to my two children who have both helped and encouraged me in my writings and my research into the lives of the rogues who donned royal robes and were the kings of the Southern Kingdom of Judah and the Northern Kingdom of Israel in Old Testament times:

My daughter, Rebekah, who loves to hear about the problems that her 'old dad' has discovered when studying the lives of the Old Testament kings and how he has found solutions to them and incorporated these into his writings.

My son, Jonathan Paul, who once paid me one of the highest compliments anyone has ever paid me—that I never taught him *what* to think; I taught him *how* to think.

May God bless you as you read about more rogues in royal robes.

Dr A J Monty White
South Wales

1 King David—first king on the throne of David

In this chapter, I want us to remind ourselves how the Israelites ended up living in the land of Canaan, being ruled over by the Royal House of David. To do this we have to go back to about 2000 BC to what is referred to as 'the call of Abraham'—the time when God called Abraham to leave his home in Haran and take his family to live in the land of Canaan. God promised Abraham that if he did this, then God would bless him and his descendants abundantly. Abraham obeyed God, and the Lord blessed Abraham and his family, and they began to prosper in the land of Canaan. The Israelites were named after the descendants of the twelve sons of Jacob, who was the son of Isaac, who in turn was the son of Abraham. Jacob was therefore the grandson of Abraham—this explains why often, in the Bible, the Israelites considered themselves to be 'children of Abraham'. Although his name was initially Jacob, the Lord changed it to *Israel*. Because of a severe famine in the land of Canaan, Jacob and his entire family eventually moved to Egypt, where one of Jacob's sons, Joseph, was a senior administrator second only to the Pharaoh. Joseph was a great grandson of Abraham and had actually been sold into slavery by his brothers because they were jealous of him. God, however, had his hand upon him and Joseph had risen to this pre-eminent position in Egypt and, as a result, he was able to help Jacob's now large family settle into the land of Goshen on the eastern side of the Nile delta, which was the best land in Egypt suitable for both crops and livestock. Here in Egypt, the Israelites, as the descendants of Jacob were now called, prospered—thus fulfilling God's promise to Abraham that He would bless his descendants abundantly.

Then, a Pharaoh came to the throne who, as the Authorised King James Version (AKJV) of the Bible puts it, 'knew not Joseph' (Exodus 1:8). It was some 400 years after Joseph had been in charge of Egypt and it would appear that this new king of Egypt knew nothing about how Joseph had saved Egypt from the effects of famine by storing food during the years of plentiful harvests and had helped Egypt become rich by selling its food to the surrounding nations, under Joseph's guidance, when the countries were suffering from famine. Furthermore, this new Pharaoh was worried about how many Israelites there were in Egypt and he considered them to be a threat to his country's security if ever Egypt was invaded. As a result, he enslaved the Israelites and even instituted a programme of genocide, commanding the midwives who looked after the Israelite mothers to kill any baby boys that were born but to allow the baby girls to live. The Bible informs us, in Exodus 1:17, that the midwives feared God and they did not obey the King but let the baby boys live. They even lied to the King, telling him that the Hebrew women gave birth more quickly than the Egyptian women and that their babies were already born before they got to the Israelite women to help deliver their babies.

Eventually, under Moses' leadership, God led the Israelites out of the land of Egypt after sending a series of plagues on the land and people of Egypt. The tenth and last of these plagues was the killing of the first-born. God told Moses about this tenth and last plague and informed him that the Israelites could escape it by sacrificing a male lamb and sprinkling its blood on the doorposts and lintels of their houses. By doing so, the Lord would pass over their homes without killing any of the first-born of their households. This was the first Passover and in his first epistle to the church in Corinth, the apostle Paul reminded his readers that the Lord Jesus Christ is our Passover Lamb sacrificed for us (1 Corinthians 5:7). Just as the Passover lambs were slain, so the Lord Jesus Christ was slain. And just as the blood of the Passover lambs had to be applied to the doorposts and lintels of the houses of the Israelites in order for them to be saved from the judgement of the Lord, so the blood of the Lord Jesus Christ has to be applied to our lives in order for us to be saved.

Moses led the Israelites out of Egypt and through the Red Sea and then, because of their unbelief and lack of trust in the Lord, they spent forty years wandering in the wilderness until there was a new generation of Israelites who trusted God. However, during these wilderness years, God did not forsake Israel—he miraculously provided them with water to drink and manna and quails to eat. Under the leadership of Joshua, the Israelites entered the so-called 'Promised Land'—the territory from the east bank of the Jordan Valley right up to the Mediterranean coast, the area we know today as Israel and Palestine.

It took about fifty years or so for the Israelites to gradually defeat the Canaanites, who occupied the land at the time. The story of how the children of Israel conquered and settled into the land of Canaan is complex and is covered in the books of Joshua and Judges. This phase of Israel's history has been ably summed up by Brian Edwards[1] as follows:

This was a messy and miserable period during which the unhappy cycle of events was that tribes squabbled among themselves, broke the laws of God and suffered the penalty. Periods of oppression by their enemies were interspersed with periods of peace led by one of the eighteen judges including the well-known figures of Deborah, Gideon and Samson.

The book of Judges in the Bible ends with the sentence: 'In those days there was no king in Israel. Everyone did what was right in his own eyes' (Judges 21:25).

Israel demands a king

The first book of Samuel opens with the story of the birth, and the subsequent calling, of Samuel to be a prophet (that is God's mouthpiece) to the nation of Israel. Towards the end of Samuel's ministry, the Israelites asked Samuel if, instead of having God ruling over them, they could have a king, like the other nations had. This was fulfilling what God said would happen. When the Lord gave the Law to Moses in the Wilderness, it is recorded in Deuteronomy 17:14 that the Lord told Moses, after Israel had taken possession of the Promised Land and had settled into it, they would decide to have a king like all the nations round about them. In other words, the nation of Israel would want to change from being a theocracy to being a monarchy. God had already warned them through the prophet Samuel that a king would take their sons for his army, their daughters for his household, the finest of their servants, their fields, their sheep, their vineyards and olive groves, and a tenth of their farm produce. In other words, the kings would indeed be rogues in royal robes—hence the phrase found in the title of this book and the title of my previous book. In 1 Samuel 12:19, it is recorded that the people soon realized they had sinned by asking God for a king but, in spite of this, God did not refuse their request.

In the Law (see Deuteronomy 17:15), the Lord had instructed Moses that the man chosen to be king of Israel was to be the one whom the Lord chose. Under God's guidance, Samuel anointed Saul as the first king of Israel. But Saul was, in fact, also the people's choice—he was the son of a wealthy farmer of the tribe of Benjamin and he was very handsome and stood head and shoulders above everyone. However, the good looking and tallest person is not always the best candidate for the job, as Samuel and the Israelites were to find out to their cost. Even at the beginning of his reign King Saul behaved badly and sinned against the Lord and, even after being reprimanded by Samuel the prophet, he did not learn his lesson but continued to sin against the Lord and blatantly lied to Samuel as well. No wonder King Saul and his lineage were rejected from being the royal kingdom of Israel.

King Saul—Israel's first king

No information about when King Saul began to reign and/or for how long he reigned is given in the books of Samuel. However, for those like me who are keen to determine such facts about this particular king of Israel, it is possible to determine the dates of the reign of King Saul from the information given in Acts 13:21, where we are informed that he reigned for forty years. We know that his successor, King David, began his reign in 1010 BC, hence we are able to determine that King Saul reigned from 1050 to 1010 BC. Reading the first book of Samuel, we can see that King Saul committed three major sins during the course of his reign that made the Lord angry with him and resulted in the Lord rejecting King Saul and seeking a man after the Lord's own heart to rule His people.

King Saul's first sin occurred right at the beginning of his reign, when the prophet Samuel told King Saul to go to Gilgal and to wait for him for seven days. Then Samuel would join him and offer sacrifices at Gilgal. King Saul obeyed Samuel and went to Gilgal but, in the meantime, the Philistines had gathered a large force at Michmash, some 12.5 miles (20 kilometres) away, and launched such a strong attack upon the Israelites that some of them hid in caves and holes in the ground and among the rocks and in pits and wells. Some even crossed the River Jordan into the territories of Gad and Gilead. Meanwhile, King Saul remained at Gilgal and he waited there for seven days for Samuel to arrive, as he had been instructed. The people, however, started to leave him, so King Saul offered a burnt offering as a sacrifice to the Lord. Now, only members of the priestly tribe of Levi were allowed to offer sacrifices; King Saul was a member of the tribe of Benjamin and, as such, he was not allowed to offer such a burnt sacrifice. In doing so, King Saul showed a complete disregard for God's Law. The prophet Samuel arrived just as King Saul was finishing offering the burnt sacrifice and he was furious. He told King Saul in no uncertain terms that what he had done was wrong!

However, King Saul did not learn his lesson and he did not repent of his sin, for he later sinned against God a second time. In 1 Samuel:15, we read the story of the prophet Samuel telling King Saul that God was going to use him and his army to punish the Amalekites for what their ancestors did by opposing the Israelites when Moses was leading them out of Egypt. Samuel told King Saul to attack the Amalekites and to destroy *everything* that belonged to them. He was told to put to death men and women, children and infants, cattle and sheep, camels and donkeys. (1 Samuel 15:3). As I pointed out in my book *Rogues in Royal Robes,* it must be understood that this was not ethnic cleansing but ethical or moral cleansing. King Saul and his army defeated the Amalekites and, although God's instructions through the prophet Samuel were abundantly clear, King Saul did not obey the Lord's command for he did not kill the King (Agag). He also allowed his soldiers to keep the best sheep and cattle, along with anything else that they considered to be good and therefore worth keeping for themselves, and he allowed them to destroy what was useless and worthless. King Saul, then, actually lied to Samuel by saying that he had obeyed the Lord's command when he manifestly had not! This resulted in Samuel telling King Saul that the Lord had rejected him as king of Israel!

King Saul's third sin occurred at the end of his reign when the Philistines made war with Israel and assembled at Shunem, which is a few miles north of the Valley of Jezreel, while King Saul led his army to Mount Gilboa on the south side of the Valley of Jezreel. When King Saul saw the Philistine army, he was terrified and he asked the Lord what to do. The Bible informs us that the Lord did not answer him by the usual methods that God used in those days—dreams, the use of Urim and Thummim[2] or prophets. Now, after the prophet Samuel had died, King Saul did do one thing that was commendable—he forced all the mediums and spiritists to leave Israel (1 Samuel 28:3). But, because King Saul was not getting an answer to his prayer, he committed an unforgivable sin: he consulted a witch—something which was punishable by death under the Law (Leviticus 20:27). He asked his officials to find a medium—a witch—who still lived in Israel and who he could consult and could answer his prayer. One such person was a witch who lived in the village of Endor. King Saul disguised himself and visited this witch and Samuel appeared to King Saul to tell him again that the Lord had taken the kingdom away from him. Furthermore, Samuel told him that on the following day, King Saul and his sons would be killed in battle—and this is what happened. King Saul was seriously wounded in a battle with the Philistines that took place the day after he had consulted the witch and he committed suicide by throwing himself on his own sword, thus ending the life of the first king of Israel.

David—shepherd boy anointed as king

Without doubt, King David was Israel's most important king with his kingdom symbolizing the embodiment of Israel's power and influence during the nation's Old Testament history. The second half of the first book of Samuel, all of the second book of Samuel and the entire first book of Chronicles are devoted to telling the story of King David's reign. Almost half of the Psalms are credited to him and in the New Testament he is identified as an ancestor of the Lord Jesus Christ. King David was the youngest son of Jesse, a farmer who lived in Bethlehem, about 5 miles (8 kilometres) south of Jerusalem. Jesse could trace his ancestry back to Judah, one of the sons of Israel (1 Chronicles 2:3–12) and he could also trace his ancestry to Ruth, who was from the land of Moab (Ruth 1:4; 4:13–17).

Until the 1990s, King David was only known from the Bible. However, in 1993, excavations at Tel Dan in the north of Israel uncovered an inscribed stone, erected by a king of Damascus in the late 9th/early 8th centuries BC to commemorate his victory over two enemy kings. This stone has the inscription *BYTDWD* on it and this has been translated 'house of David'. This inscription dates from the 9th century BC, as it had been sealed off by a later Assyrian destruction layer that has been firmly dated to 733/32 BC. This is incontrovertible proof that King David is not some mythological monarch from the dim and distant past but a real king who existed in history and that his kingdom was known about by those who lived shortly after the time that he did.

However, practically nothing is known about King David's early life except that he looked after the sheep on his father's farm in Bethlehem. We know from the conversation he had with King Saul before he killed the Philistine giant Goliath, recorded in 1 Samuel 17:34–36, that he had killed lions and bears which had attacked his father's flock of sheep. We also know that he was a well-known, accomplished musician. For, when King Saul asked his servants to find someone who could be brought to him to help soothe his black moods, immediately one of his servants recommended David and he joined the King's royal court to be what we might call these days 'the king's harpist in residence'. The only other thing we know about King David from this time is that the prophet Samuel saw he was ruddy—in other words, he had red hair—and that he had a beautiful or fair countenance and was handsome (1 Samuel 16:12).

Incredibly, David was anointed King of Israel by the prophet Samuel while King Saul was still on the throne. The prophet Samuel had been instructed by God to anoint a king from Jesse's family and, as a result, when Samuel arrived at Jesse's home all of the older sons were on hand to meet him hoping that he would anoint one of them to be king. However, the Lord told Samuel that 'man looks on the outward appearance, but the Lord looks on the heart' (1 Samuel 16:7) and the Lord revealed to Samuel that he had not chosen any of these older sons of Jesse to be anointed as king. Samuel then asked Jesse if he had any other sons. Jesse explained to Samuel that there was one other—David—but he was keeping the sheep. David was sent for and when he came in, the Lord revealed to Samuel that David was the one he had chosen to be king and that Samuel was to anoint him with the oil he was carrying. This he did and then departed while David returned to look after his father's sheep.

David—harpist, slayer of giants and fugitive

It was soon after David had been anointed by the prophet Samuel that King Saul began to suffer with his black moods and David was employed in Saul's court to play his harp to soothe Saul's melancholy. Although David was 'the king's harpist in residence', his official title was one of King Saul's armour-bearers (1 Samuel 16:21). David divided his time between King Saul's court at Gibeah (which is about 3.5 miles [5.5kms] north of Jerusalem) and his father's sheep at Bethlehem (which is about 6 miles [10kms] south of Jerusalem). But it was not as the harpist who soothed King Saul's black moods for which David became famous—it was the killing of Goliath and the subsequent defeat of the Philistine army in the valley of Elah[3]. The army of the Philistines and the army of the Israelites faced each other across the valley ready to fight each other. However, Goliath, a giant of a man and the leader of the Philistines, issued a challenge: the battle was to be decided in a single combat—Goliath versus someone chosen from the Israelite army. Young David heard Goliath's challenge when he was visiting the camp of the Israelites while taking provisions to his three eldest brothers who were soldiers in the army. David was surprised that no one from the Israelite army took up the challenge from this 'uncircumcised Philistine' (1 Samuel 17:36)—as David called him—so he begged King Saul to allow him to go. It is when he was pleading with King Saul that we learn David had defended his father's sheep from attacks by lions and bears and had killed such wild animals in his youth.

Reluctantly, King Saul allowed David to fight Goliath and he did so, using a sling. Now the sling that David used was not a child's toy sling but a formidable weapon. Slingers are shown, for example, on the Lachish reliefs that are now in the British Museum in London. These were originally on the walls of the southwest palace of the Assyrian King, Sennacherib, in Nineveh and they depict the siege by the Assyrian army in 701 BC of Lachish—a town about 25 miles (40kms) southwest of Jerusalem. It is believed that skilled slingers could project smooth stones the size of tennis balls at 100–150 mph (about 160–250 kph), so the story of David using a sling to project a smooth stone that penetrated Goliath's unprotected forehead is indeed very plausible. The result was that the Philistine army retreated, followed by the Israelites who then plundered their camp. David took Goliath's sword and cut off his head and took it to Jerusalem where he buried it. According to a footnote to Mark 15:22 in the Passion Translation of the Bible[4] the words 'Goliath' and 'Golgotha' (which means 'Skull Hill') are taken from the same root word and some believe that this is how the place where the Lord Jesus Christ was crucified got its name.

The Israelites rejoiced that the Philistines had been defeated and the women of Israel danced in the streets with their tambourines and other musical instruments and sang:

> Saul has struck down his thousands,
> and David his ten thousands (1 Samuel 18:7).

This infuriated King Saul and made him very jealous, and from then onwards he did all he could to harm David. King Saul tried to kill David twice by throwing his javelin at him, while he was comforting him by playing music on his harp, but each time David evaded death by avoiding the javelin. King Saul made David a commander of a thousand men in his army and promised him his daughter, Merab, in marriage. But King Saul then gave Merab to another man instead of David as he had promised. King Saul then promised David that he could have his daughter, Michal, as his wife, for she loved David. However, King Saul demanded a dowry—one hundred Philistine foreskins! He asked for these in the hope that David would be killed by the Philistines as he attempted to kill so many of them. However, David went with his men and between them they killed not *one* hundred, but *two* hundred Philistines, and so, David brought not one hundred, but two hundred Philistine foreskins to King Saul so that he could become the King's son-in-law.

There is no doubt that, when David was first summoned to King Saul's court to sooth the King's depression, King Saul liked him. This was before David had killed Goliath and before King Saul had heard the women of Israel singing his praises, which had caused his affection to turn into jealousy. As we have seen, this intense jealousy that King Saul had for David eventually resulted in his hating David and wanting him dead. David felt unsafe in the King's court and, in the end, he had to run for his life and become a fugitive, with the help of his relatives and about four hundred men. But King Saul would not rest until David was dead and he relentlessly pursued David with an army of some three thousand men; yet King Saul never caught him. Incredibly, without King Saul's knowledge, David had two opportunities to take King Saul's life, but he did not do so because David refused to harm him as King Saul was 'the Lord's anointed' (1 Samuel 24:6). Eventually, King Saul decided to abandon his pursuit of David and concentrated his efforts on defeating the Philistines; but he failed to do so and lost his life as a result—as we have seen.

Even with all the detail of King David's life given in the books of Samuel, it is difficult to determine the exact chronological details of his life and reign. We know that after King Saul died in 1010 BC, there followed a kind of civil war between the followers of David and the followers of King Saul. David was anointed by the leaders of Judah and he reigned in Hebron while Ish-bosheth, the son of King Saul, reigned over the rest of Israel in Mahanaim[5]. Abner, who had been the commander of King Saul's army and had been responsible for appointing Ish-bosheth as the king, eventually deserted him. He went to Hebron and met with David and pledged Israel's support for him. As he was leaving Hebron, however, Abner was murdered by Joab, a commander in David's army. Joab did this out of revenge because Abner had killed Asahel, one of Joab's brothers, in a battle at Gibeon a few years earlier. Soon after Abner's murder, Ish-bosheth was assassinated by two of his captains and, as a result, all the tribes of Israel recognized David as king over the whole of Israel and subsequently David was anointed king over all Israel at Hebron. In 2 Samuel 5:4–5, we are informed that David was thirty years old when he began to reign and that he reigned a total of forty years—over Judah at Hebron for seven and a half years and over all Israel and Judah at Jerusalem for thirty-three years. The dates of his reign were 1010 BC to 970 BC.

When David became king of the whole of Israel, the Philistines became alarmed and they twice attacked King David and his army. Although King David defeated them, he realized that he needed a good, strong, central location for his capital and he chose Jerusalem, a Jebusite stronghold. Although he built a magnificent palace for himself there, the Lord forbade him to build a Temple for the Lord—the Lord arguing that David was a man of war and that he wanted his Temple to be built by a man of peace. So, King David made plans for his successor, his son Solomon, to build the Temple. He drew up plans for the Temple and outlined the details of how the religious worship was to be conducted in it. King David stockpiled materials so the Temple could be built after his death and he also organized his kingdom for the efficient use of domestic and foreign labour that could be used in the building of the Temple.

Although King David was a great military commander and a great administrator, when it came to his own personal life, this was a disaster. King David was an adulterer who covered up his love affair by arranging for the husband of his lover to be killed in battle. Furthermore, in family matters, he failed completely to discipline his sons and to take control and organize his family affairs. As a result, he ended up with a totally dysfunctional family in which there was incest, murder and conspiracies by two of his sons to seize the throne from their father. We shall first look at King David's adultery with Bathsheba and his attempt to cover it up by murder. In the next chapter, before we look at the life of King Solomon, we shall look at the incestuous relationship that King David's son Amnon had with his own half-sister Tamar and as a result how Amnon's full-brother, Absalom, killed him and tried to become king instead of his father, David. We will then look at how King David's undisciplined son, Adonijah, tried to become king instead of King David and instead of King David's chosen successor, Adonijah's half-brother, Solomon.

David and Bathsheba

David's adultery with Bathsheba took place after King David had established himself as king over the United Kingdom of Israel in the newly established capital city, Jerusalem. It was springtime and Israel was at war with the Ammonites, but King David had stayed at home and put his army under the command of Joab. The war with the Ammonites was going well—the Israelite army had captured almost all of the territory of the Ammonites and was besieging their capital city, Rabbah[6]. King David took a stroll on his palace roof after taking an afternoon nap and he saw a very beautiful woman taking a bath. Being king, he sent servants to find out who this woman was and requested his servants to bring her to him. King David made love to her and then sent her home. This beautiful woman was Bathsheba and she was the wife of Uriah, the Hittite, who was fighting in the Israelite army against the Ammonites. It was not long before Bathsheba realized she was pregnant and she sent a message to King David to let him know.

The story of King David's adultery with Bathsheba is recorded in 2 Samuel 11. David's panic when he found out that Bathsheba was pregnant, the way he tried to cover up his being responsible for her pregnancy and how he tried to arrange for it to appear as though Bathsheba's husband, Uriah, had made her pregnant is told very vividly in that same chapter. First of all, King David sent a message[7] to Joab, the one in charge of the Israelite army, for Uriah to be dispatched to King David, who was still in Jerusalem. Joab did so and after King David had enquired of Uriah regarding how Joab and the army were and how the battle was going, the King told Uriah to go home and rest[8]. King David was hoping that Uriah would do so and sleep with Bathsheba and so it would appear that Uriah had made her pregnant. But Uriah did not go home; instead, he slept at the palace gate with the King's guards. When King David heard about this, he asked Uriah why he had not gone home. Uriah replied that he could not do such a thing when Joab, his officers and the soldiers of Israel had to camp out in the open. King David then invited Uriah to dine with him that evening. Uriah did so and King David got him drunk; but still Uriah did not go home to his wife and again slept in the palace guardroom.

The next morning, King David wrote a letter to Joab instructing him to put Uriah in the front line where the fighting was heaviest and then retreat and let him be killed. He gave the letter to Uriah to deliver to Joab. This is what Joab did and Uriah, the Hittite, was killed as instructed by King David. After Bathsheba had mourned for her husband, the King took her into his palace as his wife and she had a son. But, as the last verse of 2 Samuel 11 recalls, 'the thing that David had done displeased the Lord' (2 Samuel 11:27). As King David was soon to find out, you may be able to hide your sin from those around you, but you cannot hide it from God.

In order to confront him about his sin, the Lord sent his prophet, Nathan, to King David to tell him a story about two men—one who was very rich and had many flocks and herds and the other, who was poor, had just one little ewe lamb that he adored. Nathan told King David how the rich man had a guest come and stay with him and that, in order to feed his guest, the rich man was unwilling to take a lamb from his own flock, but took the poor man's little ewe lamb, killed it and cooked it for his guest to eat. King David did not realize that this story was a parable being spoken against him and he was furious, saying that the rich man deserved to die and that he should compensate the poor man fourfold for what he had done because he had shown no pity on the poor man. At this point, the prophet Nathan simply said to King David 'You are the man!' (2 Samuel 12:7). But Nathan had not finished. He went on to say that God had anointed him king over Israel, that He had delivered him from the hand of King Saul, and that He had given him many wives. Yet, King David had despised and disobeyed the Word of the Lord (meaning the Lord's Commandments) in that he had committed evil by committing adultery with Uriah's wife, Bathsheba, and that he was responsible for the murder of Uriah so that he could have Bathsheba as his wife. No wonder King David responded by saying, 'I have sinned against the Lord' (2 Samuel 12:13). King David further acknowledged that he had sinned against the Lord in his Psalm of Repentance when he wrote of his adultery with Bathsheba: 'Against thee, thee only, have I sinned, and done this evil in thy sight' (Psalm 51:4) [King James Version].

We know that King David really did repent of his adultery, for we can see this in the famous words that he penned, again in his Psalm of Repentance: 'Create in me a clean heart, O God; and renew a right spirit within me' (Psalm 51:10) [King James Version]. However, the son who was the result of David and Bathsheba's adulterous affair, died in spite of David's fasting and praying for a whole week that he might live. But, remarkably, King David and Bathsheba had another son whom they called Jedidiah which means 'beloved of the Lord'— he is known to all by his other name: Solomon.

Summary and conclusion

For all his faults, and King David had many as we have seen, we can see that he was without doubt a great king of Israel. He was a mighty warrior, a great leader and a fine poet, even though he was an adulterer and a murderer. But how should we remember him? What has he left us? I believe that he has left us four great inheritances. The first is a great City, Jerusalem, which, in spite of its being severely damaged many times, still stands today as a testimony and memorial to King David who first established it as the capital of Israel. The second is a great temple, Solomon's Temple. Although King David's son, King Solomon, actually built it, King David was its chief architect and the one who outlined the details of how the religious worship was to be conducted in it. King David stockpiled materials so the Temple could be built after his death and he organized the Kingdom of Israel for the efficient use of domestic and foreign labour to help with the construction of the Temple. Unfortunately, Solomon's great Temple was destroyed by the Babylonian army in 586 BC, so we shall never be able to see it in all its glory. King David's third great inheritance that he has left us is 73 great psalms, written some three thousand years ago but so many of these strike a chord with the same human feelings that we experience today. And finally, King David's fourth great inheritance is a great royal throne, the Throne of David on which David's greater son, the Lord Jesus Christ, sits and reigns forever and ever.

Before we leave this section about King David, let us remind ourselves of what is perhaps David's most well-known psalm—the twenty third psalm, which in the Authorised King James Version of the Bible reads as follows:

> The LORD is my shepherd; I shall not want.
> He maketh me to lie down in green pastures:
> > he leadeth me beside the still waters.
> He restoreth my soul:
> > he leadeth me in the paths of righteousness for his name's sake.
> Yea, though I walk through the valley of the shadow of death,
> > I will fear no evil:
> > for thou art with me;
> > thy rod and thy staff they comfort me.
> Thou preparest a table before me in the presence of mine enemies:
> > thou anointest my head with oil;
> > my cup runneth over.
> Surely goodness and mercy shall follow me all the days of my life:
> > and I will dwell in the house of the LORD for ever.

This Psalm was composed by David when, perhaps, he was still a young man tending his father's sheep near Bethlehem. It captures the Lord keeping watch over us, his sheep, and leading us, feeding us and caring for us all the days of our life, as the Lord did for David all the days of his life.

3 Chapter 1

NOTES

1 Brian, H. Edwards, *Saul and Sons, Decline and fallout in the family of Israel's first king,* (Leominster: Day One Publications, 2010). pp.5–6.

2 Urim and Thumimm are two untranslated Hebrew words which might mean 'lights and perfections'. They refer to some kind of stones or tokens which the High Priest of Israel used for discovering the will of God. Theories abound but most guess that they were something like dice or coins which had to land upright or upside down as an answer to prayer.

3 For details of where the Valley of Elah is located, see https://bibleatlas.org/valley_of_elah.htm

4 *The Passion Translation, New Testament with Psalms, Proverbs, and Song of Songs,* Second Edition, (Savage, Minnesota: Passion & Fire Ministries Inc., Broad Street Publishing, 2018).

5 The exact location of Mahanaim is uncertain, but it is thought to be about 10 miles (16 kms) east of the River Jordan, near the Jabbok River. See https://en.wikipedia.org/wiki/Mahanaim

6 The ancient site of Rabbah is now covered by Amman, the capital city of modern Jordan.

7 At the time, it would appear that the Israelite army was besieging Rabbah, the capital city of the Ammonites and this was some 45 miles (72 kilometres) from Jerusalem. Assuming this message was taken from King David to Joab by foot, it would have taken a couple of days for Uriah to walk from Rabbah to Jerusalem. Sometimes we are not aware of the distances involved in the Bible stories and we forget that the individuals we are reading about had to walk from place to place—they did not have cars or public transport! Furthermore, when they sent messages to each other, they did not have email or mobile phones to do so—they had to walk from one place to another in order to give or take a message.

8 In the King James Version, the New International Version and the English Standard Version of the Bible, it is recorded that King David told Uriah to go home and 'wash [his] feet' (2 Samuel 11:8). Since this washing was done before going to bed, this idiom meant, 'Go home and go to bed', and, as pointed out by John MacArthur in his Study Bible, to a soldier coming from a battlefield this idiom said boldly, 'Go home and enjoy your wife sexually.' MacArthur, John, *The esv MacArthur Study Bible,* (Wheaton, Illinois: Crossway, 2010), p. 438.

Chapter 1

NOTES

1 Brian, H. Edwards, *Saul and Sons, Decline and fallout in the family of Israel's first king,* (Leominster: Day One Publications, 2010). pp.5–6.

2 Urim and Thumimm are two untranslated Hebrew words which might mean 'lights and perfections'. They refer to some kind of stones or tokens which the High Priest of Israel used for discovering the will of God. Theories abound but most guess that they were something like dice or coins which had to land upright or upside down as an answer to prayer.

3 For details of where the Valley of Elah is located, see https://bibleatlas.org/valley_of_elah.htm

4 *The Passion Translation, New Testament with Psalms, Proverbs, and Song of Songs,* Second Edition, (Savage, Minnesota: Passion & Fire Ministries Inc., Broad Street Publishing, 2018).

5 The exact location of Mahanaim is uncertain, but it is thought to be about 10 miles (16 kms) east of the River Jordan, near the Jabbok River. See https://en.wikipedia.org/wiki/Mahanaim

6 The ancient site of Rabbah is now covered by Amman, the capital city of modern Jordan.

7 At the time, it would appear that the Israelite army was besieging Rabbah, the capital city of the Ammonites and this was some 45 miles (72 kilometres) from Jerusalem. Assuming this message was taken from King David to Joab by foot, it would have taken a couple of days for Uriah to walk from Rabbah to Jerusalem. Sometimes we are not aware of the distances involved in the Bible stories and we forget that the individuals we are reading about had to walk from place to place—they did not have cars or public transport! Furthermore, when they sent messages to each other, they did not have email or mobile phones to do so—they had to walk from one place to another in order to give or take a message.

8 In the King James Version, the New International Version and the English Standard Version of the Bible, it is recorded that King David told Uriah to go home and 'wash [his] feet' (2 Samuel 11:8). Since this washing was done before going to bed, this idiom meant, 'Go home and go to bed', and, as pointed out by John MacArthur in his Study Bible, to a soldier coming from a battlefield this idiom said boldly, 'Go home and enjoy your wife sexually.' MacArthur, John, *The esv MacArthur Study Bible,* (Wheaton, Illinois: Crossway, 2010), p. 438.

2 King Solomon—fame and fortune

K ing Solomon's father, King David, died at the age of seventy in 970 BC after reigning over Israel for forty years. Towards the end of his life, King David addressed the leaders of his kingdom in Jerusalem and reminded them that the Lord God of Israel had chosen him to be king over Israel and that the Lord had also chosen his son Solomon to sit on his throne after his death (1 Chronicles 28:4–7). In an earlier chapter, the Lord had spoken to King David and told him that Solomon would be God's son, that God would be his father, and that God would establish his royal throne in Israel for ever (1 Chronicles 22:10). Thus, the royal throne of David was established and its continuance assured. In those days, the idea that the king should be succeeded by his eldest son was not taken for granted—the king expected the Lord to make the decision of who would succeed him when he died. Hence King David was succeeded by Solomon, who was not his firstborn son, but the son that both the Lord and King David had chosen to succeed him when he died.

Absalom—one of David's spoilt brats!

Although King David was a brilliant military leader and diplomat, we have already seen that, in his own personal life, he did not show any moral backbone and not only did he commit adultery with Bathsheba, but he arranged to have her husband, Uriah the Hittite, killed in battle in order to try to cover up his sin. Unfortunately, King

Chapter 2

David showed the same lack of moral fibre in disciplining his sons and keeping his own house in order. When his eldest son, Amnon, committed incest by raping his half-sister, Tamar, although King David was angry with Amnon, he actually did nothing whatsoever to discipline him for doing such an evil and wicked thing to Tamar, who was not only Amnon's half-sister but also one of King David's own daughters. However, Tamar's full-brother, Absalom, was furious at what Amnon had done to her and for two whole years he did not speak to Amnon but plotted somehow to punish him for what he had done to Tamar. After the two-year period, Absalom held a sheep-shearing party to which he invited all his brothers, including Amnon. Absalom instructed his servants to watch Amnon carefully and he commanded them to murder Amnon when he had had too much to drink. When Amnon's brothers saw that he had been killed, they rushed from the party to tell their father, King David, what had happened. So that he could escape any punishment that his father might bestow upon him, Absalom sought safety in Geshur—an independent city state located in the region of the modern-day southern Golan Heights, which at the time was ruled by King Talmai, who was the father of Absalom's mother, Maacah, and so was also Absalom's grandfather.

For the next three years, Absalom lived in safety in Geshur because both he and his sister, Tamar, were members of the royal family through their mother, Maacah. However, King David missed Absalom very much and, through Joab, arrangements were made for him to return from exile to Jerusalem. However, when Absalom returned home, King David refused to meet him and refused to allow him to live in the King's palace. It was two years before King David would allow Absalom to meet him and when he did, he did not admonish him for arranging for his brother Amnon to be murdered, but actually welcomed him with a kiss. Absalom was now the eldest son and he began to desire his father's throne. For the next four years Absalom campaigned tirelessly for it by getting up early in order to meet and greet the ordinary people who had come to Jerusalem to have their grievances and disputes settled. By doing so, he obtained increasing support from the people and this was helped by the fact that Absalom was very good-looking with long thick hair.

Sometimes when we read the Bible, timelines and therefore the time scales involved, can easily escape our attention. Perhaps at this juncture it will be good to remind ourselves of the timeline and the time scale of the story of Absalom. It was two years after his half-brother Amnon raped Tamar that he arranged for Amnon's murder. Absalom then lived with his mother's relatives in Geshur for three years before returning home. It was two years later that King David met him and then he spent four years meeting and greeting the people who went to Jerusalem with their grievances and disputes. This makes a total of eleven years between the time that Amnon raped Tamar and the time that Absalom made his attempt to seize the throne from his father.

Absalom had managed to keep King David in the dark about the coup d'état he was about to attempt in order to take the throne from his father. Absalom asked King David if he could go to Hebron on the pretext that, while he was in exile in Geshur, he had made a promise to the Lord that if the Lord took him back to Jerusalem, then Absalom would go to Hebron and worship him there. King

David agreed to Absalom's request but Absalom sent messengers to all the tribes of Israel to tell them that, when they heard the sound of trumpets, they were to shout, 'Absalom is king at Hebron!' (2 Samuel 15:10). When King David and those who were faithful to him heard that the children of Israel were pledging their support for Absalom, they managed to escape from the palace in Jerusalem and reach the River Jordan just as Absalom and his army were entering Jerusalem. King David found reinforcements for his army from his friends and allies who lived on the other side of the River Jordan and this larger army eventually defeated Absalom's rebel army. Absalom, himself, was killed as he was trying to flee on his mule when his head was caught in the branches of a large oak tree and he was left hanging in mid-air. Joab and ten of his soldiers then killed him with their weapons while he was hanging in the branches of the oak tree. When King David was informed of Absalom's death, he mourned for Absalom and wished that he had died in his place. King David returned to Jerusalem and eventually gained control over his kingdom after the rebellion led by his son Absalom. In the next section we shall see that, because King David had not disciplined his children, it was not only Absalom who tried to become king in his place. We shall see that another of David's undisciplined sons, Adonijah, tried to become king before his father had died and also instead of Solomon, who was King David's, as well as the Lord's, named successor.

Adonijah—another one of David's spoilt brats!
We have seen that King David's son, Absalom, was what we would call today 'a spoilt brat', for his father never disciplined him even

when he arranged for his half-brother, Amnon, to be murdered. Furthermore, we have seen the chaos that occurred in King David's life and in the life of the nation of Israel as the result of Absalom thinking he could do as he pleased and even take the throne from his father. But Absalom was not the only son of King David who was a spoilt brat, for we read in the Good News Version of 1 Kings 1:6, that King David had never reprimanded his son, Adonijah, about anything. As a result of this, Adonijah was just like his brother, Absalom, and was ambitious to be King David's successor—even when King David was on his deathbed. Adonijah was Solomon's half-brother and King David had already determined that Solomon should be his successor when he died. But Adonijah was having none of this. At the beginning of the first Book of Kings we read that Adonijah persuaded Joab, the commander of his father's army, and Abiathar the priest to support his cause. In order to achieve this, Adonijah went to a place called Snake Rock which is located inside modern Jerusalem and offered a sacrifice of sheep, bulls and fattened calves. He invited the other sons of King David—this would be his brothers and half-brothers—and the King's officials from Judah to attend this sacrificial feast, but he did not invite his half-brother, Solomon, Nathan the prophet, Benaiah, or King David's bodyguard. The reason for this is that, as we have already seen, King David had already chosen his son, Solomon, as his successor and Nathan the prophet, Benaiah, and the King's bodyguard were not on Adonijah's side—neither were Shimei, Rei or Zadok the priest.

Nathan the prophet[1] then went to Bathsheba, who was Solomon's mother, and informed her of this insurrection by Adonijah and enquired if King David knew about it. Bathsheba and Nathan then informed King David about how Adonijah had made himself king and how the people were proclaiming him as king. As a result, King David instructed Zadok the priest, Nathan, Benaiah and his court officials to take Solomon to the spring of Gihon, which is on the eastern slope of Mount Zion, and there, Zadok and Nathan anointed Solomon 'King of Israel' with oil taken from the sacred tent that David had erected in Jerusalem to house the Ark of the Covenant. They blew the trumpet and the people who were there shouted 'Long live King Solomon!' (1 Kings 1:39), and they then began to return to King David's residence playing flutes and shouting for joy. Adonijah and his guests were just finishing their feast when they heard the noise that the people were making about King Solomon being made king and, as a result, Adonijah feared for his life. He made his way to the sacred tent that King David had erected and grabbed hold of the horns of the altar that was housed in it, trusting that King Solomon would not have him put to death while he held onto these horns. King Solomon promised that, if Adonijah were loyal to him, then not even a hair on his head would be touched, but if he was not loyal to him, he would die. After this, King Solomon told Adonijah that he could go home.

But that is not the end of the story of Adonijah. After King David died, Adonijah went to see Bathsheba, King Solomon's mother, and requested her to ask King Solomon if he could marry Abishag. The story of Abishag is found in 1 Kings 1:1–4. It is a straightforward story. King David was a very old man—seventy years old—and was having problems in keeping warm. It was decided that, to help him keep warm, a search of the kingdom should be made and a beautiful young virgin should be chosen to look after him and also lie close to him in his bed to keep him warm. Abishag was chosen for this purpose.[2] It is emphasized in the story that King David did not have sexual relations with Abishag and she remained a virgin. Bathsheba acquiesced to Adonijah's request and asked King Solomon if Adonijah could marry Abishag. King Solomon was absolutely furious with what Adonijah had asked and he gave orders that Adonijah should be executed that very day. This execution was carried out by Benaiah, who, as we have already seen, was present when Solomon was anointed king. Perhaps Adonijah would have behaved very differently if his father, King David, had disciplined him when he was growing up and made him realize that he could not have everything he wanted. As a result, maybe Adonijah would not have tried to be king instead of his half-brother, Solomon, and maybe Adonijah would not have lusted after Abishag and tried to have her as his wife when his father died.

The wisdom of Solomon

Soon after becoming king, Solomon called all the leaders of Israel to join him at Gibeon, which is about 5 or 6 miles (8 to 10 kilometres) northwest of Jerusalem and there on a bronze altar, which was located in front of the Tent of the Lord's presence,[3] King Solomon sacrificed a thousand animals. That night, the Lord appeared to King Solomon and asked him what he would like the Lord to give him. King Solomon asked for wisdom and knowledge so that he could rule God's people, Israel, sensibly. The Lord granted King Solomon's wish and, in addition, promised him wealth, riches and honour.

It was not long into his reign that King Solomon was asked to judge a difficult case and his judgement was such that his wisdom spread throughout his kingdom and is still referred to today (1 Kings 3:16–28). Two prostitutes lived with each other. One of them gave birth to a baby boy and, two days later, the other prostitute also gave birth to a baby boy. Only the two women and their babies lived in the house. Let one of the women take up the story:

> One night, the prostitute I live with accidentally rolled over onto her baby and smothered it. She got up during the night and took my son from my side while I was asleep and carried him to her bed and then she put the dead child in my bed next to me. The next morning when I awoke and was going to feed my baby, I saw that it was dead. I looked at it more closely and saw that it was not my child (author's own version).

The other woman protested saying that the young child was hers and that the dead child was the other woman's baby. The first woman replied that the dead child was the other woman's and the living child belonged to her. And so, they quarrelled before King Solomon. This is when King Solomon used the wisdom that God had given him. He asked for a sword and said, 'Cut the living child in two and give half to one and half to the other' (1 Kings 3:25, NIV). The real mother, her heart full of love and compassion for her son, begged for his life and asked King Solomon not to kill her son but to give him to the other woman. The other woman, however, showed no love for the child but said, 'Neither I, nor you, shall have him. Cut him in two! (v. 26, NIV). King Solomon then knew who the real mother was and commanded that the child be given to the first woman who was the child's real mother.

God not only promised Solomon great wisdom, which he exhibited in his judgement concerning who was the actual mother of the child, but he promised him wealth and honour. Solomon's wealth was revealed to the Queen of Sheba when she visited him and she tested his wisdom by asking him many difficult questions—all of which he was able to answer. But she was left breathless and amazed when she saw the living quarters of his palace staff and the uniforms they wore and the food that was served at his table. She exclaimed that she had not heard half of it before her visit! Solomon's wisdom is well-known, even to this day. His wealth and honour were also well-known—even a thousand years later the Lord Jesus Christ referred to 'Solomon in all his glory' (Matthew 6:29 [AKJV & ESV]).

The apostasy of Solomon

In spite of his wisdom, wealth, honour and glory, King Solomon had a huge problem. I have heard it said on many occasions that Christian leaders fall down in one of the following three areas: Fame, Finances or Females.[4] You only have to look at the history of some of the charismatic (and not so charismatic) leaders on the television 'God channels' over the last thirty to forty years to observe this. The ones that have been seen to fall have done so as a result of one or more of these three Fs. *Fame*: the overwhelming craving of wanting the limelight for themselves and not wanting the praise and glory for the Lord. *Finances*: the taking of huge amounts of money for themselves (sometimes totally illegally) and thereby living in unbelievable luxury. *Females*: the committing of adultery by having affairs or visiting prostitutes. It is in one or more of these three areas that pastors, deacons and elders of churches from whatever denomination or theological persuasion, whether large or small, have to be continually on their guard. It is rather ironic that it was Solomon who, some three thousand years ago, wrote that 'there is nothing new under the sun' (Ecclesiastes 1:9).

In addition to wisdom, the Lord gave Solomon fame *and* finances. But Solomon was not satisfied. He had to have females—and lots of them! Although the Old Testament nowhere forbids polygamy, in Deuteronomy chapter 21, rules are given concerning men who take a woman captive in war and also about men who have more than one wife. We must remember that in the beginning God made one wife (Eve) for the first man (Adam). We must also remember that God made one bride (the church) for His only begotten Son. In the Law, the king is commanded not to acquire many wives for himself (Deuteronomy 17:17). Yet, King Solomon took polygamy to excess and broke that command, for he married 700 princesses and, in addition, he had 300 concubines! And the result of this was that these women made him turn away from God and caused him to worship foreign gods. King Solomon's father, King David, in committing adultery with Solomon's mother, Bathsheba, and subsequently murdering her husband, broke several of the Ten Commandments; but King Solomon broke the First Commandment big time when he built places of worship where all his foreign wives could burn incense and offer sacrifices to their own gods.

Furthermore, on the hill to the east of Jerusalem, which would later be called the Mount of Corruption, King Solomon built two places of worship—one to worship Chemosh, the god of the Moabites and the other to worship Milcom (or Molech as he was also called), the god of the Ammonites. This latter place of *so-called worship* was a place where child sacrifice was practised—a place where children were thrown alive into a heated bronze animal (usually depicted as a bull). The screams of the babies and the young children as they were being sacrificed were drowned out by the beating of drums and the playing of musical instruments so that their parents could not hear them. In the Law, the Lord had forbidden the Israelites to sacrifice their children to Molech ('passing through the fire to Molech' as it was called, Leviticus 18:21, kjv) and the Israelites had all but wiped out this practice when they conquered the Canaanites and occupied the Promised Land. Yet here was King Solomon re-introducing child sacrifice and this practice continued until King Josiah's reign over 300 years later (see 2 Kings 23:10).

Solomon's Temple

The other remarkable thing for which King Solomon is known is Solomon's Temple—the Temple that he built to house the Ark of the Covenant, the tent in which the Lord God dwelt. King David wanted to build a permanent place for the Ark of the Covenant. He was well aware that when the children of Israel lived in tents in the Wilderness, God lived in a tent, but now that the Israelites lived in houses in the Promised Land, King David thought that God should dwell in a house—a Temple specially built for him. Let us not forget that, at the dedication of the Temple, King Solomon reminded the people of Israel (and through the pages of Scripture we, too, are reminded) that the heavens, even the highest heavens cannot contain God. Yet a building specially built to house the Ark of the Covenant was what King David wanted and this was what the Lord God graciously allowed. The Lord explained to King David, however, that because he was a man of war, he was not to build the Temple; this task was to be undertaken by his son, Solomon, when he became king as he would be a man of peace because God would give peace to Israel during his reign. Yet, King David not only had plans drawn up for the Temple (which he gave to his son, Solomon), but he also stockpiled materials so the Temple could be built after his death (see 1 Chronicles chapters 22 and 29). Furthermore, King David organized the kingdom of Israel for the efficient use of domestic and foreign labour to help with the construction of the Temple and he also outlined the details of how the religious worship was to be conducted in the Temple after it had been built.

King Solomon began to build the Temple in the fourth year of his reign (2 Chronicles 3:2) and it took seven years to build it. When it was completed, the Ark of the Covenant was brought into it but before doing so, however, King Solomon and all the people of Israel who were present sacrificed so many sheep and oxen that they could not be counted or numbered (2 Chronicles 5:6). Then King Solomon dedicated the Temple in a prayer that caused the glory of the Lord to fill the Temple and fire to come down from heaven and consume a further 22,000 bulls and 120,000 sheep that were sacrificed. This caused all the people who were present to bow down with their faces to the ground and to worship and give thanks to the Lord. Solomon's Temple, as it was called, remained in existence for almost 400 years until it was destroyed by King Nebuchadnezzar and his Babylonian Army in the summer of 586 BC.

Summary and conclusion

Although at the beginning of his reign, King Solomon had been wise and his kingdom could be described as glorious, towards the end of his reign, King Solomon was not quite so wise and his kingdom was not as glorious as it had once been. Although he was responsible for building a magnificent Temple that stood for almost 400 years, King Solomon spent twice as much time building his own palace as he had done building the Temple. As a result of marrying foreign princesses and building altars and temples for them to practise their own religion, King Solomon's heart eventually turned away from the Lord and he even introduced child sacrifice into Israel. However, even outside Christian circles, King Solomon is remembered as a wise, gifted and intelligent man—one who was knowledgeable about philosophy, nature, politics and commerce. He is also remembered as a king who ruled wisely and one who brought prosperity, peace and happiness to his people. In addition, this man was a productive author who has left us with psalms, proverbs and love songs.

We have already seen God's grace at work in the lives of the leaders of Israel and have seen his forgiveness of those who repented of their sins—even when they committed murder to cover their adultery. The study of the genealogy of the Lord Jesus Christ in Matthew's Gospel makes interesting reading as so many of Jesus' forefathers are the kings of the Southern Kingdom of Judah—about whom we will be studying in the following chapters of this book. We will see how they rebelled against the Lord and how the Lord forgave them when they repented. We will also see how the Lord blessed them when they obeyed him and, when they disobeyed him, we will see that often the Lord brought disease to them personally, famine to the land, or invasion by their enemies. But sadly, they never

learned and they ended up with their kingdom being taken captive
into Babylon after Jerusalem, together with Solomon's magnificent
Temple, had been destroyed by King Nebuchadnezzar and his army.
No wonder then, that when the children of Israel, who had been
taken captive from the Southern Kingdom of Judah, were in Babylon,
they cried:

> By the waters of Babylon,
>> there we sat down and wept,
>> when we remembered Zion.
> On the willows there
>> we hung up our lyres.
> For there our captors
>> required of us songs,
>> and our tormentors, mirth, saying,
> 'Sing us one of the songs of Zion!'
> How shall we sing the Lord's song
>> in a foreign land?
>
>> (Psalm 137:1–4)

NOTES

1 This was the same prophet Nathan who had exposed David's adultery with Bathsheba and the subsequent murder of her husband, Uriah the Hittite, so that David could marry her.
2 My wife used to call Abishag 'a human hot water-bottle'.
3 The Ark of the Covenant resided at Jerusalem in a tent (1 Chronicles 15) awaiting the building of the Temple, while the Mosaic tabernacle and altar remained in Gibeon until the Temple was completed (1 Kings 8:4).
4 I have also heard these three referred to as *Glamour, Gold or Girls* and *Popularity, Possessions and Pleasure.*

3 King Rehoboam—foolish loser

When we read the history of the Israelites recorded in the books of Kings and Chronicles, sometimes God tells the king what was going to happen—usually via one of his prophets. Often this was a result of the king 'enquiring of the Lord', so he knew what was going to happen and so he could work out what to do. If the king was not happy with what he was told, he often did all he could physically do to ensure that it did not happen. But what God told the king would happen *always* happened, no matter what the king did in order to try to stop it. The only exceptions to this were when the king prayed earnestly that God would not do what he said he was going to do; when the king repented of the action he was about to take; or when the king repented of sin that was in his life. One obvious example of this was in the case of King Hezekiah, after the prophet Isaiah had told him he was about to die. He prayed earnestly that God would heal him and, as a result, fifteen years were added to his life (see 2 Kings 20:1–7).

A good example of a king doing all he could physically do in order to try to stop God's Word being fulfilled was when King Ahab of the Northern Kingdom of Israel was told by the Lord, via his prophet Micaiah, that he would die in battle if he went to war against the Syrians (1 Kings 22:19–22). However, King Ahab was determined to go to war against the Syrians so he could regain control of the city of Ramoth Gilead, which was within the territory of his kingdom and which had been taken over by the Syrians.

Furthermore, King Ahab asked King Jehoshaphat of the Southern Kingdom of Judah to join him in the battle to retake control of Ramoth Gilead. As they prepared for the battle, King Ahab suggested that King Jehoshaphat dress in his royal robes and that he, Ahab, would dress as an ordinary soldier. We can see clearly that King Ahab hoped, as a result of this, the Syrians would attack and kill King Jehoshaphat because he was dressed in his royal robes and that they would not attack King Ahab because he did not dress in his royal robes and looked like an ordinary soldier. But when the Syrian soldiers attacked King Jehoshaphat and heard him speaking, they realized that he was not King Ahab and so stopped attacking him. However, King Ahab was struck 'at random' according to the ESV translation (1 Kings 22:34)—'by chance' according to the Good News Bible—by a Syrian's arrow between the joints in his armour and this caused him to collapse and bleed to death in his chariot.

This story about King Ahab is a good illustration of to what extraordinary lengths people, even kings, will go in order to try to stop the Lord's words being fulfilled. By giving this one example we see that, no matter how hard people try, they cannot stop God's Word from coming to pass unless, of course, they pray earnestly that God would have mercy upon them and not do what he said he would do; they repent of the action they are about to take; or when they repent of sin that is in their lives. There are instances, however, when people accept what the Lord says, even when he has predicted that some very unpleasant and disastrous events will take place—this is what happened when King Solomon died and a civil war occurred in the Kingdom of Israel with devastating and unforeseen consequences. However, before Solomon died God had already told him that his kingdom would be split in two during the reign of his son (1 Kings 11:9–13). King Solomon did not argue with God and accepted what the Lord said would happen. The main characters (King Solomon's son, Rehoboam, and his rival, Jeroboam) involved in this civil war both accepted that the war that ensued between the southern tribes and the northern tribes of Israel and the subsequent split of the United Kingdom of Israel into the Southern Kingdom of Judah and the Northern Kingdom of Israel was God's will. Furthermore, King Rehoboam desisted from going to war with the Northern Kingdom of Israel when the Lord told him not to do so by the prophet Shemaiah, who also told him that the split of the Kingdom of Israel into two was God's will (1 Kings 12:24).

(For the sake of clarity, in this book I have called Israel before the split, either *Israel* or *the United Kingdom of Israel*, and I have called Israel after the split, the *Northern Kingdom of Israel*, and I have called Judah, *the Southern Kingdom of Judah*. However, to complicate matters even further, the Bible sometimes calls the Northern Kingdom of Israel, *Samaria*, after the city that became the capital city of the Northern Kingdom in the reign of Omri.)

Who was Rehoboam?

Scripture tells us a great deal about King Rehoboam's life and also about his family and who was related to whom within his family. However, Rehoboam is the only named son of Solomon[1]—in fact, the Bible only records the name of *three* of Solomon's children: his son, Rehoboam, and his two daughters, Basemath and Taphath.

Furthermore, the Bible does not record how many children Solomon had, in spite of the fact that he had 700 wives and 300 concubines! However, this should not surprise us for the writers of the books of Kings and Chronicles did not usually compile a complete list of the names of wives, daughters or sons—occasionally they would record the name of a favourite wife (or wives) and usually they would record the name of the heir, and sometimes, but not always, the name of the heir's mother. They would often record the names of the important or favourite sons or daughters of the king. This can be seen clearly in the family tree of Rehoboam reproduced on page 53. He had eighteen wives, sixty concubines and he fathered eighty-eight children—twenty-eight sons and sixty daughters. However, the names of only seven of his sons and only two of his wives are actually recorded in the Bible—see 2 Chronicles 11:18–21.

If Solomon did have only one son, Rehoboam, this could be due to genetics. We know that the gender of a baby depends on whether the father's sperm carries an X or a Y chromosome. If the father's X chromosome combines with the mother's X chromosome, then the child will be XX—a girl; but if the father's Y chromosome combines with the mother's X chromosome, then the child will be XY—a son. If for some reason Solomon produced sperm that had very few Y chromosomes, then this would explain why Solomon had only one son—Rehoboam. Most of his children would then have been girls. The days when men thought that it was their wives who were responsible for the gender of the child to which they gave birth are (or should be) long past because we now know from genetics that the gender of a child depends on his or her father, not the mother.

Rehoboam's mother was Naamah and she was an Ammonitess and

52 More Rogues in Royal Robes

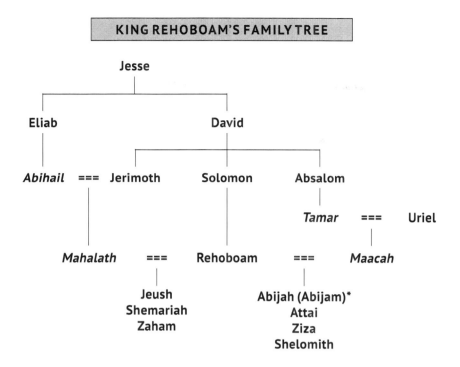

KING REHOBOAM'S FAMILY TREE

Jesse

Eliab — David

Abihail === Jerimoth — Solomon — Absalom

Tamar === Uriel

Mahalath === Rehoboam === *Maacah*

Jeush
Shemariah
Zaham

Abijah (Abijam)*
Attai
Ziza
Shelomith

*This son of Rehoboam is called Abijah in 2 Chronicles and Abijam in 1 Kings.

so was one of the 700 foreign wives that King Solomon married and who were princesses. Although not mentioned specifically in the Bible, Naamah was presumably a princess of the royal house of Ammon, a kingdom which was to the east of Jerusalem. In fact, apart from her name, from where she came and the name of her husband and son, we know nothing else about Naamah for the Bible is silent about her life, or indeed, her ancestry. One interesting observation in a piece of writing about Naamah points out that the Bible refers to her as 'the Ammonite'[2] and that this is 'in much the same way as Marie Antoinette was referred to [by the French of her day] as "the

Austrian"—a disparaging title summing up the hostility of the common people to a marriage between their king [Solomon] and a princess from a country [Ammon] that they distrusted.' However, in the Jewish Encyclopaedia we are informed that:

> In the second Greek account (I Kings xii.24) Naamah is said to have been the daughter of Hanun, son of Nahash, a king of Ammon (II Sam. x. 1-4).[3]

This would make sense because Hanun's father, King Nahash of Ammon had befriended King David and helped him and so it would not be unreasonable for King Hanun's daughter (the Princess Naamah) to marry Rehoboam who was King David's grandson.

Rehoboam was forty-one years old when he ascended the throne and he reigned for seventeen years from 930 to 913 BC. He was therefore fifty-eight years old when he died. As we have already noted, we are informed in 2 Chronicles 11:21 that King Rehoboam had eighteen wives and sixty concubines and that he fathered twenty-eight sons and sixty daughters, yet the names of only two of his wives and only seven of his sons are actually mentioned in the Bible and these are shown in the family tree on page 53. In this family tree, I have shown Abihail, the daughter of Eliab being married to Jerimoth, the son of David and half-brother of Solomon. This is following the information found in 2 Chronicles 11:18 in modern translations of the Bible (for example the NIV, ESV and GNT). In the AKJV, however, this verse is translated in such a way that it gives the impression that Rehoboam, not Jerimoth, was married to Abihail. Unfortunately, this is the way that Robert Young has interpreted this verse in his famous Concordance where it states under entry number 4 for Abihail that she was 'a daughter of Eliab David's brother, and wife of Rehoboam'.[4]

It is worth looking carefully at Rehoboam's family tree, which is reproduced on page 53. This family tree has been drawn up using the information in 2 Chronicles 11:18–22 found in the New King James Version where it states that Maacah is the granddaughter of Absalom; in most other translations it states that Maacah is the daughter of Absalom. In 2 Chronicles 13:2, it states that the father of Maacah (spelled Micaiah in this verse) is Uriel of Gibeah. Such statements have led some to believe the Biblical accounts of Rehoboam's family to be contradictory. However, such apparent contradictions disappear completely with a study of Hebrew linguistics. One of these apparent contradictions is that Maacah is described as the daughter of Absalom and sometimes as the daughter of Uriel. In 2 Samuel 14:27, we are informed that Absalom had one daughter, Tamar, who was incidentally 'a beautiful woman'. Josephus proposed that Tamar was the mother of Maacah and that she was married to Uriel.[5] Now, in Hebrew, 'daughter' and 'granddaughter' are the same word, removing any contradiction in 2 Chronicles 11:20 where it refers to Maacah as being the daughter of Absalom when in actual fact she was his granddaughter. Similarly, Maacah is initially described as Abijah's mother in 2 Chronicles 11:20, but subsequently she is depicted as the mother of his son Asa in 2 Chronicles 15:16 (KJV). In Hebrew, however, the word for 'mother' and 'grandmother' are the same, as already stated, so once again any apparent contradiction is removed.

The family tree also highlights some of the relationships that resulted in people marrying within their own family. First of all, we can see that Rehoboam was Jesse's great grandchild and that he married Mahalath who was also a great grandchild of Jesse, and he also married Maacah who was a great, great grandchild of Jesse. We can also see that Rehoboam was David's grandson and that his wife Mahalath was a granddaughter of David and the other wife Maacah was a great granddaughter of David. Rehoboam and his wife Mahalath were therefore cousins and Rehoboam and his wife Maacah were second cousins. Mahalath and Maacah were also second cousins. However, because Solomon, Jerimoth and Absalom had different mothers, technically all these cousins were in fact half-cousins. With his wife, Mahalath, Rehoboam had three sons: Jeush, Shemariah and Zaham. And with his wife, Maacah, Rehoboam had four sons: Abijah (aka Abijam), Attai, Ziza and Shelomith. We are informed that of all his wives and concubines, King Rehoboam loved Maacah the most and that he favoured her son Abijah (aka Abijam) over all his children and chose Abijah to succeed him as the king of the Southern Kingdom of Judah (2 Chronicles 11:21–22).

King Rehoboam—idiot of this parish!

To understand fully how and why there was a civil war soon after King Rehoboam became king, we have to go back a few years and learn about Jeroboam, who became one of King Solomon's senior administrators. He is introduced to us in chapter eleven of the first book of Kings, where we are told that he was one of King Solomon's officials; that his father's name was Nebat; that he was from Zeredah in Ephraim; and that his widowed mother was named Zeruah. At the time, Jeroboam was working for Solomon helping to fill in the land on the east side of Jerusalem and assisting with the repair of the city walls. Solomon was very impressed by how hard Jeroboam worked and as a result he put him in charge of all the forced labour in the territories of the tribes of Ephraim and Manasseh. This made a lot of sense because Jeroboam was from Zeredah in the tribal territory of Ephraim.

Because of King Solomon's idolatry, the Lord sent the prophet Ahijah to Jeroboam, who at the time was travelling alone from Jerusalem and was in open country. Ahijah was wearing a new robe and he took it off and tore it into twelve pieces. He then commanded Jeroboam to take ten pieces and told him that the Lord was going to take the kingdom away from King Solomon. However, he would not do this while he was living, but would do this when his son reigned. The prophet Ahijah also told Jeroboam that the Lord would give him ten of the tribes of Israel to rule over. The prophet then instructed Jeroboam that when he was king, he was to keep God's commandments and if he did so, the Lord would bless him and his descendants would rule after him. Somehow, King Solomon heard about this prophecy, even though it was delivered on an open road in open country and where apparently there was no-one around to hear it! There are, however, many instances where the sound of a person's voice travels over great distances. Although I do not have the reference, I once read an account of a farmer ploughing his field and thinking about how he could get right with God. He then heard the answer: that he was to repent of his sins and trust the Lord Jesus Christ as his Saviour. The words that he heard were actually spoken by John Wesley who was preaching to a crowd in the open air well over a mile away! So, there are instances where people's voices travel over huge distances and therefore, we can only assume this is what happened when Ahijah was prophesying to Jeroboam and that whoever heard it told King Solomon. As a result, King Solomon tried to kill Jeroboam—presumably he thought that if he could do this, the Word of the Lord delivered to Jeroboam by Ahijah the prophet would not come to pass. But Jeroboam escaped to Egypt and stayed there under the protection of King Shishak until King Solomon's death. In the Septuagint, we are informed that on Jeroboam's departure from Egypt, with the permission of King Shishak, he married Ano who was the older sister of Shishak's wife[6]—thus Jeroboam became Shishak's brother-in-law.

King Solomon died of natural causes at the age of about sixty in 930 BC and his son Rehoboam became king of the United Kingdom of Israel. We read in the Scriptures (1 Kings 12:1) that Rehoboam went to Shechem where all the people of northern Israel had gathered to make him king—in other words, Rehoboam was going to have his coronation at Shechem. When Jeroboam heard about this, he returned from his self-imposed exile in Egypt and the people of the northern tribes, led by Jeroboam, then met with King Rehoboam and requested that the high taxes and the forced labour for the nation's building projects, which had been imposed upon them by his father King Solomon, be reduced. They said that if this was done, they would be his loyal subjects and would serve him. King Rehoboam asked for three days to consider their requests. During this time, King Rehoboam first consulted the older men who had counselled his father, King Solomon, and they advised him to give a favourable response to the people's request saying that, in doing so, the people would serve him loyally. It is not at all clear whether these elderly counsellors actually recommended the King accept the people's demands.

King Rehoboam, however, ignored the advice of the old men and instead turned to the young men who had grown up with him and who were now his counsellors. He asked them how he should respond to the people and they answered with those well-known words found in 1 Kings 12:10–11 (NIV):

> My little finger is thicker than my father's waist.
> My father laid on you a heavy yoke; I will make it even heavier.
> My father scourged you with whips; I will scourge you with scorpions.

And this, believe it or not, is what King Rehoboam answered the people when they returned to him after three days. I have called King Rehoboam, 'idiot of this parish', in the heading of this section because he was, without doubt, an absolute idiot to take on board the advice given to him by the young men with whom he had grown up. If he had taken the opinion of the older men who had counselled his father, he could have had the children of Israel eating out of his hand, as the saying goes. However, as a consequence of what he said to them, about 30% of the people[7] rebelled, with the result that the northern tribes rallied around Jeroboam, crowned him as their king and started a new kingdom—the Northern Kingdom of Israel. The two tribes in the south of Israel—Judah and Benjamin—remained loyal to King Rehoboam and formed the Southern Kingdom of Judah.

Sometimes people think that events which happened in the history of Israel somehow 'caught God out' and God did not see them coming. If people think this with regard to the civil war that occurred in Israel and the split of the United Kingdom of Israel into the Northern Kingdom of Israel and the Southern Kingdom of Judah, then they could not be further from the truth. As we noted above, God had already told King Solomon directly and he had also told Jeroboam via the prophet Ahijah, that the United Kingdom of Israel was going to be split into two. When he told Jeroboam via the prophet Ahijah, he also informed him that he, Jeroboam, would rule ten of the tribes. Furthermore, the Lord informed King Rehoboam very clearly through the prophet Shemaiah that this civil war and the resulting split of the United Kingdom of Israel was from God, and that King Rehoboam was forbidden to try to recapture the Northern Kingdom of Israel from King Jeroboam I (see 1 Kings 12:22–24). However, it must be said that what happened, as a result of this civil war, did cause massive problems for the children of Israel, as we saw in my previous book[8] and as we shall also see in this book.

The majority of the children of Israel broke away from the United Kingdom of Israel and formed their own kingdom with its own monarchy and called this newly established kingdom, Israel. Because the new kingdom was called Israel, it does cause confusion when reading the books of Kings and Chronicles. When you follow the story closely, you realize that, before the civil war, the whole Kingdom of Israel was called Israel. The civil war caused a split which resulted in two separate kingdoms—Israel and Judah.

Consequences of the civil war in Israel

First of all, let us remind ourselves how the descendants of Israel came to be living in the Promised Land at the time of the civil war in Israel. The patriarch Abraham lived about four thousand years ago and his grandson, the patriarch Jacob, who was later renamed Israel, had twelve sons. As a result of a severe famine in the land of Canaan where Jacob and his family were living, Jacob and his entire family moved to Egypt where one of his sons, Joseph, was the senior administrator second only to the Pharaoh. Joseph had actually been sold into slavery by his brothers because they were jealous of him. God, however, had his hand upon Joseph's life and he had risen from being a slave to this pre-eminent position in Egypt and so he was able to help Jacob's now large family (who were all related to him, remember) settle into the land of Goshen on the eastern side of the Nile delta, which was the best land in Egypt suitable for both crops and livestock. Here in Egypt, the Israelites, as the descendants of Jacob were now called, prospered and during the 400 years that they lived there, they grew in number. And, because they tended to marry within their family, each son gave rise to a tribe and each of these tribes was given an area in the Promised Land after leaving Egypt under the leadership of Moses. However, each of Joseph's sons, Ephraim and Manasseh, were given their own tribal area (instead of Joseph having one), and to complicate matters even further, Levi was not given any tribal area—members of the tribe of Levi were scattered throughout the land because they were priests with what could be described as civic as well as religious duties.

It is easy to think of there being twelve tribes of Israel and that the civil war in the United Kingdom of Israel in 930 BC resulted in there being a ten-two split, thus fulfilling Ahijah's prophecy to Jeroboam that he would rule over and be king of ten of the tribes of Israel. However, it was a little more complicated than that—it often is, as I have tried to explain in this and my other book about the history of the Israelites and the kings who reigned over them.[9] One of the complications that we have to confront, and about which we have to be clear, is that although there were twelve tribes of Israel, because Ephraim and Manasseh, the two sons of Joseph, were each given a tribal area, sometimes it appears there were *thirteen* tribes of Israel! In the table on the page 63, I have listed Joseph's sons, Ephraim and Manasseh, separately and thus it appears that there are indeed thirteen tribes of Israel. Because of this, the table shows that the civil war did not result in a ten-two split, but a nine-four split (with some taken away from the nine and some added onto the four). This in no way contradicts what Ahijah said to Jeroboam. He told him that he would rule over ten tribes and he actually did so until the members of the tribe of Levi left the Northern Kingdom of Israel and moved into the Southern Kingdom of Judah. This was because King Jeroboam had rejected them as priests of the Lord once he set up his own religion.

The table on page 63 shows the distribution of the tribes of Israel in the Northern Kingdom of Israel and the Southern Kingdom of Judah after the civil war. It can be seen that it was not only members of the tribe of Levi that 'packed their bags', so to speak, and moved from their homes in the Northern Kingdom of Israel down into the Southern Kingdom of Judah, but so did those from every other tribe of the Northern Kingdom of Israel who 'set their hearts to seek the Lord God of Israel ... the God of their fathers' (2 Chronicles 11:16). This explains why, in the New Testament, we read of people in Judea (which is the Roman name for the Southern Kingdom of Judah) being descended from one of the tribes that were from the Northern

TABLE SHOWING THE DISTRIBUTION OF THE TRIBES OF ISRAEL IN THE NORTHERN KINGDOM OF ISRAEL AND THE SOUTHERN KINGDOM OF JUDAH AFTER THE CIVIL WAR	
The Northern Kingdom of Israel	**The Southern Kingdom of Judah**
Asher	Judah
Dan	Benjamin
Ephraim	Simeon*
Gad	Levi—all the Levites abandoned their
Issachar	homes and property in the Northern
Manasseh	Kingdom of Israel and moved south
Naphtali	to the Southern Kingdom of Judah
Reuben	because King Jeroboam I had
Zebulun	rejected them as priests of the Lord
	as soon as he set up his own religion
	(2 Chronicles 11:13–14).
	and
	Those from every other tribe of Israel
	who set their hearts on seeking the
	Lord, the God of Israel, the God of
	their fathers (2 Chronicles 11:16).

*The area occupied by the tribe of Simeon was south of that occupied by the tribe of Judah which in turn was south of the area occupied by the tribe of Benjamin. Simeon was a very small tribe and got smaller with the passage of time. It was always located in the Southern Kingdom.

Kingdom of Israel. An obvious example is Anna—the old widow in the Temple in Jerusalem who was the daughter of Phanuel from the tribe of Asher and who, when she saw the baby Jesus. realized who he was and told people about him (see Luke 2:36–38).

Rehoboam and archaeology

After the civil war, King Rehoboam set about establishing his authority as king. One of the first things he did was to fortify a number of the towns and cities in the Southern Kingdom of Judah and to appoint a commander in each of them, after which he placed supplies of food and weapons there. He also put some of his sons in these fortified towns and cities as well. In all probability he did this because he thought that, as a result of the civil war and the continuing disputes between him and King Jeroboam I of the Northern Kingdom of Israel, that his kingdom would be invaded and conquered by Shishak, King of Egypt, who was, remember, the brother-in-law of King Jeroboam I. The Southern Kingdom of Judah, however, actually became stronger as a result of the actions taken by King Jeroboam I in the Northern Kingdom of Israel, for he built places of worship on hilltops and appointed priests from families who were *not* of the priestly tribe of Levi. Because of these actions, the Levites abandoned their homes and property in the Northern Kingdom of Israel and moved south to the Southern Kingdom of Judah. The Bible informs us in 2 Chronicles 11:16 that people from other tribes who were in the Northern Kingdom of Israel and who wanted to worship the Lord sincerely also moved to the Southern Kingdom of Judah with the Levites. These people from the north supported King Rehoboam and lived as they and their ancestors had done, under the reigns of King Solomon and his father, King David. What was King Jeroboam's loss was, in fact, King Rehoboam's gain and it strengthened the Southern Kingdom of Judah.

However, after three years, King Rehoboam showed his true colours and revealed what a rogue he really was when he abandoned the Law of the Lord. We see over and over again, not only in Biblical times but also today, that the children of God-fearing parents often abandon the ways of the Lord. The Bible informs us that although King Rehoboam retained Jerusalem with Solomon's Temple as his capital, the inhabitants of the Southern Kingdom of Judah became more and more idolatrous and 'they built places of worship for false gods and put up stone pillars and symbols of Asherah to worship on the hills and under shady trees' (1 Kings 14:23, Good News Translation) and 'worst of all, there were men and women who served as prostitutes at those pagan places of worship' (1 Kings 14:24, GNT). No wonder then that in the fifth year of King Rehoboam's reign—in the spring of 925 BC to be precise[10]—his kingdom was invaded by King Shishak of Egypt. The Lord sent the prophet Shemaiah to King Rehoboam to tell him that he had abandoned God and now God was abandoning him!

Although this king of Egypt is called Shishak in the Bible, he is identified by Egyptologists as Pharaoh Shoshenq I (or Sheshonq I or Sheshonk I—all three spellings are used), a Libyan who was the founder of Egypt's 22nd dynasty. He reigned from 943 to 922 BC so the years of his reign show that he was a contemporary of King Rehoboam. The Bible records in 2 Chronicles 12:3–4 that Shishak's army was composed of one thousand two hundred chariots, sixty thousand horsemen and more soldiers than could be counted, including Libyan, Sukkite and Sudanese troops and that they captured the fortified cities of the Southern Kingdom of Judah and advanced as far as Jerusalem. This invasion is not only recorded in the Scriptures, but it is also recorded by the Egyptians on the famous Bubastite Portal which is in the temple of Amun in Karnak. At the time of my writing about this particular invasion[11], the images and the writings on this portal at Karnak illustrate the earliest account of an event that is described in the Bible for which there is an extra-Biblical source. On this now-weathered portal at Karnak, we can see a depiction of King Shishak holding a group of captives by their hair and striking them with his mace. Below him and behind him are the names of the Canaanite towns and cities that he and his army conquered or destroyed. While the identification of some of these places is uncertain and others are now unreadable (due to almost three thousand years of weathering) some of these names—Ajalon, Beth Shan, Beth Horon, Gibeon, Megiddo and Socoh—are clearly legible and are towns and cities that were located in the territories of the Southern Kingdom of Judah and the Northern Kingdom of Israel and these towns and cities are all named in the Bible.

Furthermore, a fragment of a stela bearing the cartouche[12] of Shoshenq I (Shishak, as he is known in the Bible) was found in Megiddo in 1926. Dr Rupert Chapman[13], a retired curator and administrator in the Middle East Department of the British Museum, has concluded that the original stela was erected during Shishak's presence in Megiddo and that it probably stood in front of one of the major public buildings there. Following Shishak's return to Egypt, the stela was defaced and broken up and that the so-called *Shishak fragment* (on which his name [cartouche] is carved) was then used as building material for almost three thousand years until it was discovered in 1926. The finding in Megiddo of a fragment of a stela on which Shishak's name is carved is testimony of this Pharaoh's successful campaign in Palestine.

Noticeably absent from the Bubastite Portal is the name of

Jerusalem. There are two possible explanations for this. The first one is that the name of Jerusalem is no longer legible due to erosion as a result of almost three thousand years of weathering. The other explanation is simply that Shishak did not destroy Jerusalem. This is what Josephus implies when he states that Shishak took the city without fighting and, after King Rehoboam had received him, Shishak then looted the treasures of the Temple and of the King.[14] Now this is in complete agreement with the account of Shishak's invasion of the Southern Kingdom of Judah, which is found in 2 Chronicles 12:1–12 where we read that Shishak advanced as far as Jerusalem but there is no mention of his destroying the city—only that he took treasures from the Temple and from the King's palace. This was probably the tribute that King Rehoboam agreed to pay Shishak in order to save Jerusalem from destruction. One interesting fact the Bible records is that Shishak took from the Temple the golden shields that King Solomon had had made and that King Rehoboam replaced them with brass shields (in the sunlight they would glint and shine and have the appearance of being made of gold) which he entrusted to the officers who guarded the palace gates. Every time King Rehoboam went to the Temple they were put on display, presumably to deceive the people, who would be worshipping with the King in the Temple, that Solomon's golden shields were still housed there and had not been taken by Shishak. The rest of the time these shields were kept in the guardroom.

Shishak died in 922 BC and was succeeded by his son Osorkon I. After Osorkon I had been reigning for three years, he made an offering to the gods and goddesses of Egypt, details of which have been discovered on a granite pillar in a temple at Bubastis, in the eastern Nile Delta. Although only fragments of the long and detailed hieroglyphic text of Osorkon I have been found, these show that the offerings amounted to an astounding 383 tons of gold and silver.[15] There is no indication from where this gold and silver came, but as Alan Millard, Ranklin Professor Emeritus of Hebrew and Ancient Semitic Languages at the University of Liverpool, has pointed out it is reasonable to suppose that much of it was the gold that Osorkon's father, Shishak, carried away from Solomon's Temple and the King's palace at Jerusalem.[16] It is ironic to think that some of the gold that Osorkon I would have offered to his gods and goddesses would have been the same gold that was given to the Israelites by the Egyptians at the time of the exodus, when the Israelites escaped from Egypt under the leadership of Moses.

A brief history of the Northern Kingdom of Israel

In this book, I want to concentrate on the history of the Southern Kingdom of Judah and look at the lives and times of some of the kings who ruled over this kingdom. With this in mind, I think that it would be beneficial at this juncture for us to look briefly at what happened in the Northern Kingdom of Israel after its creation as a result of the civil war that we have been looking at in this chapter. As we have seen, Jeroboam I was the first king of the Northern Kingdom of Israel and when he began to reign, he realized that he had two problems to deal with—one political and one religious.

The political problem that King Jeroboam I faced was concerning which town or city to have as the capital of the Northern Kingdom of Israel. King Jeroboam I chose the city of Shechem as his first capital—Shechem was a city located in the hill country of Ephraim, north of Bethel and Shiloh on the high road going from Jerusalem to the northern districts. It was the city where King Solomon's son, Rehoboam, met with all Israel and it was where the tribes that eventually became the Northern Kingdom of Israel rebelled against Rehoboam when he refused to meet their demands to make their taxation and burdens lighter. As a result, they made Jeroboam I their king in 930 BC. A thousand years earlier, the Lord had appeared to Abraham at Shechem and had told him that the Lord was going to give that land to Abraham's descendants (Genesis 12:6–7). The Israelites had also carried the body of Joseph with them out of Egypt and had buried it at Shechem (Joshua 24:32). Today the ruins of the ancient city of Shechem, known in Arabic as *Tell el-Balata*, lie just over a mile southeast of the modern Arab city of Nablus on the northern West Bank. King Jeroboam I did not keep Shechem as his capital for very long. He soon vacated it and fortified the town of Penuel and made that city his capital instead. The city of Tirzah, in the territory of Manasseh, became the third capital city of the Northern Kingdom of Israel in the time of Jeroboam I.

The religious problem that Jeroboam I faced and one that worried him (see 1 Kings 12:25–27) was that the centre of worship for *all* the children of Israel was the Temple that was in Jerusalem—which was located in the Southern Kingdom of Judah. King Jeroboam I was afraid that if the Israelites in the Northern Kingdom of Israel crossed the border into the Southern Kingdom of Judah to visit and worship the Lord in the Temple in Jerusalem, they would transfer their allegiance to King Rehoboam, who was king of the Southern Kingdom of Judah. King Jeroboam I actually had the idea that, as a result of this transfer of allegiance, his people would kill him.

So-called *Fake News* is not a new phenomenon thought up by leading politicians and news reporters in the 21st century. King Jeroboam's solution to the problem he faced was to construct two golden calves and to place one of them in the city of Dan in the north of the country and the other in Bethel in the south of the country and to tell the people the lie that these were their gods who brought them out of Egypt! (1 Kings 12:28). King Jeroboam actually used the same words as those recorded in Exodus 32:4, after Aaron had made the golden calf for the people to worship. What an example of fake news on both occasions! And the problem was that in both instances the people believed the lie contained in this fake news. Furthermore,

TABLE SHOWING THE RELATIONSHIP WITH EACH OTHER OF THE ASSYRIAN KINGS WHO ARE MENTIONED IN THE BIBLE

The names in italics are wives or concubines.

All the dates are BC and are the actual dates that the monarchs reigned.

In Ezra 4:10, King Ashurbanipal is called Asnappar in the King James Version and Osnappar in the English Standard Version of the Bible.

Tiglath-Pileser III === *Yaba*
(745–727)

Shalmaneser V   **Sargon II** === *Ra'ima*
(727–722)   (722–705)

    Sennacherib === *Zakutu*
    (705–681)

      Esarhaddon === *Ashur-hamat*
      (681–669)

        Ashurbanipal
        (669–631)

King Jeroboam I also built places of worship on hilltops and appointed priests from families who were *not* from the priestly tribe of Levi. This reinforces the explanation given in one the sections above as to why the Levites abandoned their homes and property in the Northern Kingdom of Israel and moved south to the Southern Kingdom of Judah. As we have already seen, what was King Jeroboam's loss was definitely King Rehoboam's gain and it strengthened the Southern Kingdom of Judah.

After Solomon's death in 930 BC, the Kingdom of Assyria became increasingly powerful and, within a hundred years, King Jehu of the Northern Kingdom of Israel was paying tribute to Shalmaneser III, king of the Assyrians in 841 BC. A hundred years later, King Tiglath-Pileser III invaded the Northern Kingdom of Israel and as a consequence some of the northern tribes were taken captive to the northern border area of the Assyrian Empire. Then, for nearly three years, King Shalmaneser V, King Tiglath-Pileser III's son and successor, besieged Samaria, the capital city of the Northern Kingdom of Israel. It fell in 723 BC, the year of King Shalmaneser V's death, and his successor, his brother King Sargon II, took more of the people captive from the now defeated Northern Kingdom of Israel and moved them to the River Gozan area and to the cities of the Medes. From 721 BC onwards, King Sargon II and his successors (especially his grandson, King Esarhaddon and his great grandson, King Ashurbanipal) continued the established Assyrian policy of repopulation. (See table on page 70, showing the relationship/family tree of the Assyrian Kings.) At this time more Israelites were moved to the River Gozan area and the cities of the Medes, and the depopulated land of Israel was repopulated with foreign peoples who later became the Samaritans of the Lord Jesus Christ's time. Thus, the Northern Kingdom of Israel ceased to exist and its peoples were taken away from the Promised Land and were taken into captivity as a result of their disobedience and idolatry, just as the Lord had warned them would happen in Deuteronomy chapter twenty-eight.

The table on page 73 shows that the monarchal line in the Northern Kingdom of Israel was not from father to son, as it was in the Southern Kingdom of Judah, but was often overturned by assassinations, murders, court plots and even a suicide! During the period from 930 BC when King Jeroboam I began to reign and 723 BC when the Assyrians finally destroyed the city of Samaria which was then the capital city of the Northern Kingdom of Israel, there were nineteen kings and the line was broken eight times. In seven of these, the king was murdered by his successor, while the eighth committed suicide. The lives of these Old Testament kings of the Northern Kingdom of Israel make depressing reading and the majority of these kings led the children of Israel (God's chosen people) away from God.

A brief history of the Southern Kingdom of Judah

As we have seen, Rehoboam did not inherit his father's wisdom and, as a result of his refusing the request from the northern tribes of Israel to reduce their work and tax burdens, a civil war ensued and this resulted in the United Kingdom of Israel being split into the Southern Kingdom of Judah and the Northern Kingdom of Israel. As we shall see in this book, the kings and the people of the Southern Kingdom of Judah did not learn from their own mistakes, nor from the mistakes made by their neighbours in the Northern Kingdom of

TABLE SHOWING THE KINGS OF THE NORTHERN KINGDOM OF ISRAEL
Nine dynasties – 19 kings
• 1st Dynasty: Jeroboam I; Nadab • 2nd Dynasty: Baasha; Elah • 3rd Dynasty: Zimri • 4th Dynasty: Omri; Ahab; Ahaziah; Jehoram • 5th Dynasty: Jehu; Jehoahaz; Joash; Jeroboam II; Zechariah • 6th Dynasty: Shallum • 7th Dynasty: Menahem; Pekahiah • 8th Dynasty: Pekah • 9th Dynasty: Hoshea
Eight of these kings met their death by violence – that is 42% of them. Seven of these kings were assassinated by his successor and one committed suicide:
• Nabad was assassinated by Baasha – 1 Kings 15:27 • Elah was assassinated by Zimri while Elah was getting drunk – 1 Kings 16:9–10 • Zimri only reigned a week before committing suicide at Tirzah – 1 Kings 16:18 • Jehoram was killed by Jehu – 2 Kings 9:24 • Zechariah was assassinated by Shallum – 2 Kings 15:10 • Shallum was assassinated by Menahem – 2 Kings 15:14 • Pekahaah was assassinated by Pekah – 2 Kings 15:25 • Pekah was assassinated by Hoshea – 2 Kings 15:30

Israel—even when they saw their northern brothers and sisters being taken into captivity by the Assyrians. Not even this made them repent and turn to the Lord and serve him with all their hearts and minds. There were a few kings of the Southern Kingdom of Judah who faithfully served the Lord, but these were the exceptions rather than the rule. Three of these exceptions worth mentioning were King Jehoshaphat, King Hezekiah and his grandson, King Josiah. However, in general, the kings continued to sin against the Lord and lead the people away from serving the Lord. Yet amazingly, the monarchical line in the Southern Kingdom of Judah, which was from father to son, survived and so the Throne of David survived.

Towards the end of this book, we shall consider the history of the last twenty years of the Southern Kingdom of Judah and we shall see that this makes very sad reading. From 605 BC until 586 BC the Babylonians, led by King Nebuchadnezzar, invaded the Southern Kingdom of Judah several times. Each time not only was the land invaded, but the city of Jerusalem was also attacked and damaged by the Babylonian army and with each invasion, the Babylonians took more of the people from the Southern Kingdom of Judah captive back to Babylonia (that is, the city of Babylon and its surrounding districts). The city of Jerusalem was finally sacked on 10th July 586 BC, a hundred years after the death of their exceptional monarch, King Hezekiah. The people from the Southern Kingdom of Judah, who were taken into captivity to Babylon, began to return to their homeland some seventy years later under the Persian kings. The events surrounding the return of the people from this *Babylonian Exile* (as it became known) and the rebuilding of Jerusalem are recorded in the books of

Ezra and Nehemiah. The descendants of the people who returned from Babylon are the Jews of the New Testament.

Summary and conclusion

Although there had always been some hostility between the tribes that lived in the geographical north and the geographical south of Israel, King David had managed to unify them and they lived at peace with each other during the latter part of his reign and under the reign of his son, King Solomon. However, as soon as Solomon's son, Rehoboam became king, the hostility between the two factions erupted when the tribes from the north asked King Rehoboam to reduce their burdens—both forced labour and taxes. As a result of King Rehoboam listening to the unsound advice from his young counsellors, he told them that he was going to be much tougher than his father, King Solomon, had ever been. This led to civil war in Israel and led by Jeroboam, who became their king, this caused the tribes from the north to rebel and form their own kingdom in the northern area of Israel. When King Rehoboam formed a large army to invade the Northern Kingdom of Israel, God sent Shemaiah the prophet to tell him not to attack Jeroboam because it was God's will that this civil war, with the consequential split of the United Kingdom of Israel into two, had happened.

After the civil war, King Rehoboam ruled from his capital, Jerusalem, over the Southern Kingdom of Judah which was composed of the tribes of Judah, Benjamin, Simeon, Levi and a few people from some of the tribes of the Northern Kingdom of Israel— people who were not happy with the decisions that King Jeroboam was making about who were appointed as priests and how the people were to serve false gods. King Rehoboam established and strengthened the Southern Kingdom of Judah but, after three years, he forsook following the Lord by abandoning the Law of the Lord. This had unforeseen consequences, one of which was that the Lord abandoned his protection of King Rehoboam's kingdom and it was invaded by the Egyptians, led by their king, Shishak, who is identified as Pharaoh Shoshenq I. An account of this invasion of the land of Palestine by Shishak is found on the Bubastite Portal which is in the temple of Amun in Karnak. The images and the writings on this portal at Karnak illustrate the earliest account of an event that is described in the Bible for which there is an extra-Biblical source. Although there is no mention of Jerusalem in the account inscribed on this portal, this is probably due to King Rehoboam giving Shishak tribute in the form of gold and silver from the Temple and from his palace in Jerusalem. The result of the Egyptian invasion of the Southern Kingdom of Judah was the severing of the trade routes to South Arabia via Elath and the Negev, that had been established during King Solomon's reign. As a result of this, the Southern Kingdom of Judah became a vassal state of Egypt.

The paying of tribute to Shishak weakened the Southern Kingdom of Judah. Furthermore, the Bible informs us that during King Rehoboam's reign, the Southern Kingdom of Judah and the Northern Kingdom of Israel were constantly at war with each other (1 Kings 14:30)—this warfare further weakened the Southern Kingdom of Judah, and it also weakened the Northern Kingdom of Israel. King Rehoboam reigned for seventeen years from 930 to 913 BC and the Bible summarizes Rehoboam's life in 2 Chronicles 12:14 (GNT) with this sad epitaph:

> He did what was evil, because he did not try to find the Lord's will.

This is not a good obituary to have and unfortunately this can also be written about millions of people today. How many people really try to find God's will? Here is a lesson for us all: do we try to find God's will for our lives? It takes much prayer, Bible reading, studying and also, unlike King Rehoboam, taking note and acting upon the wise counsel of older Christians who have walked with Christ for many years. Do not be like the foolish 'idiot of this parish' (as I called King Rehoboam in an earlier section of this chapter) who did not listen to his wise, older advisers and dismissed their advice with tragic consequences.

King Rehoboam was fifty-eight years old when he died and his life was unremarkable after Shishak's invasion and was not marked with any other important event. The Bible informs us that, when he died, King Rehoboam was buried in the royal tombs in David's City and that he was succeeded by his son, Abijah, who was the son of his favourite wife, Maacah.

NOTES

1 Rehoboam is certainly the only son of Solomon mentioned in the Bible. The legendary emperor of Ethiopia, Menelik I, is reputed to have been the result of the union of the Queen of Sheba with King Solomon, but there is *no* mention of such a union in the Bible.
2 'A Foreign Wife from Ammon' in: https://womeninthebible.net/women-bible-old-new-testaments/naamah/
3 http://www.jewishencyclopedia.com/articles/11254-naamah
4 Robert Young, *Analytical Concordance to the Holy Bible. [Eighth Edition]*, (London: Lutterworth Press, 1973), p. 4.
5 As explained, the family tree on page 53 has been compiled using the information in 2 Chronicles 11:18–22 where in every translation, with the exception of the New King

James Version, it states that Maacah is the daughter of Absalom. The New King James translation states that Maacah is the *grand*daughter of Absalom. The reason for this is that in 2 Chronicles 13:2 the father of Maacah (spelled Micaiah in this verse) is given as Uriel of Gibeah. Two explanations for this are possible. One explanation is that proffered by Josephus and this is recorded on page 2117 of volume 4 of the 1997 edition of *Baker Encyclopedia of the Bible*—this is that Maacah's mother may have been Tamar, the daughter of Absalom. This would make Uriel the father and Absalom the maternal grandfather of Maacah. The other explanation is that Absalom was also known as Uriel because he was such a disgrace within the royal family. At present we simply do not know, and may never know, why two different names are given for Maacah's father. Coming from a family where people are often known by two, and sometimes even three different names, I personally have no problem with two different names being used for the same person. As an example, I had an uncle who was known as Harold (his legal name) and Wally (the name that most people called him)—he was called both names and everyone who knew him had no problem in using either of these two names when referring to him!

6 *New English Translation of the Septuagint*. 3 Reigns (Old Greek) 12:24e. [1 Kings 12:24]. Electronic version at http://ccat.sas.upenn.edu/nets/edition/

7 I have based this figure on the fact that four of the thirteen tribes rebelled: that is just over 30%.

8 A. J. Monty White, *Rogues in Royal Robes,* (Leominster: Day One Publications, 2020).

9 A. J. Monty White, *Rogues in Royal Robes*.

10 The exact year and season has been determined by: Edwin R. Thiele, *The Mysterious Numbers of the Hebrew Kings*, (Kregel, Grand Rapids, MI: Kregel, 1983), p. 80.

11 Autumn 2020.

12 A cartouche is a royal name enclosed in an oval shape.

13 Rupert L Chapman III, 'Putting Sheshonq in His Place', *Palestine Exploration Quarterly,* 141(1) (2009), pp. 4–17 reproduced at https://www.researchgate.net/publication/233585548_Putting_Sheshonq_I_in_his_Place

14 Flavius Josephus, 'The Antiquities of the Jews, Book viii, chapter x, para 3' in: *Josephus, The Complete Works, 3rd printing*, (London: Pickering & Inglis Ltd, 1964) p. 186.

15 Kenneth, A. Kitchen, 'Where Did Solomon's Gold Go?' Bible and Spade 07:4 (Autumn 1994). Part of this article is reproduced at https://www.galaxie.com/article/bspade07-4-02

16 Alan Millard, *Discoveries from Bible Times* (Oxford: Lion Publishing, 1997) p. 108.

4 King Jehoshaphat – friend of the enemy

T owards the end of his life, King David publicly prayed to the Lord and, in so doing, he addressed the children of Israel who were gathered in Jerusalem at the time. He explained to them how he had made provision for the Temple that his son Solomon would build after his demise. During this prayer, he uttered these words: 'Our days are like a passing shadow, and we cannot escape death' (1 Chronicles 29:15, GNT). These words of David were spoken some three thousand years ago and they are still true today. According to Benjamin Franklin, one of the founding fathers of the United States of America and one who helped draft the American Declaration of Independence, 'In this world nothing can be said to be certain, except death and taxes.' Although he wrote this in a letter to Jean-Baptiste Le Roy in 1789,[1] the phrase appeared previously in Daniel Defoe's book, *The Political History of the Devil*, which was published in 1726 and ten years earlier in Christopher Bullock's book, *The Cobbler of Preston*, which was published in 1716. But it is Benjamin Franklin's statement of this fact which is so well-known and which is usually attributed to him. We saw, in an earlier chapter, that King David did not escape death and we saw in the last chapter that his grandson, Rehoboam, actually refused to listen to the people when they asked for a reduction in their taxes. King Rehoboam's failure to acquiesce to his people's demands for their taxes to be reduced, caused a civil war in Israel, which resulted in a split of the United Kingdom of Israel into two smaller kingdoms: the Southern Kingdom of Judah and the Northern Kingdom of Israel. This occurred in the year 930 BC.

In this chapter, I want us to look at the life and times of King Rehoboam's great grandson, who was one of the most successful and influential kings that ruled the Southern Kingdom of Judah—King Jehoshaphat. He reigned for twenty-four actual years from 872 to 848 BC. But before we do so, I want us to look briefly at the reign of King Rehoboam's son, King Abijah (as he is known in Chronicles) or Abijam (as he is called in Kings), and then at the life and time of his son, King Asa, who was King Jehoshaphat's father.

Jehoshaphat's grandfather, Abijah

King Rehoboam died in 913 BC and he was succeeded by his son, Abijah (aka Abijam), whom he had chosen to succeed him and who was the son of his favourite wife, Maacah. We saw, in Chapter 2, the chaos that can ensue when a favourite son is not disciplined and tries to usurp his father's throne. In the case of Abijah, however, he rightly took the throne when his father, King Rehoboam, died and the record in 1 Kings 15:3 (Good News Translation) of his short reign states that 'he committed the same sins as his father and was not completely loyal to the Lord his God, as his great-grandfather David had been.' He only reigned three years (from 913 to 910 BC) and his reign was overshadowed by his constant war with King Jeroboam of the Northern Kingdom of Israel. Wars are notorious for weakening a country because the soldiers have to be paid and fed using so-called *Government money* which has to be raised in the form of taxation from the inhabitants of that country. This diversion of monies often results in any newly planned infra-structures and any new building projects of the country not being undertaken and work being stopped on those already in progress. If the country is invaded by the enemy, then there are costs in repairing the damage to the towns and cities that has resulted from such an invasion. In Biblical times, the successful invading army plundered and looted the defeated army and country and this helped to fund the army and replenish the coffers of the country that was victorious.

We saw, in the last chapter, that the Southern Kingdom of Judah was invaded by the Egyptians, led by their king, Shishak, early on in the reign of King Abijah's father, King Rehoboam. This invasion had devastating consequences on the economy and therefore the wealth of the Southern Kingdom of Judah. Shishak's army destroyed many of the towns and cities in the Kingdom and they received as tribute literally tons of silver and gold from the Temple and from the King's palace. The result of this Egyptian invasion also had a devastating effect on the infrastructure of the Kingdom as the trade routes to South Arabia, that had been established during King Solomon's reign, were severed. The severing of these trade routes, the paying of the considerable tribute to Shishak and the destruction of many of its towns and cities greatly weakened the Southern Kingdom of Judah. In addition, the continual warfare that existed between the Southern Kingdom of Judah and the Northern Kingdom of Israel during King Rehoboam's reign damaged further the already weakened state of the Southern Kingdom of Judah. As noted in the previous paragraph, this constant warfare between the Northern and Southern Kingdoms continued during the reign of King Abijah.

However, there was one event in King Abijah's short reign that helped the Southern Kingdom of Judah to regain some of the strength, power and wealth that it had lost. This event is recorded in chapter 13 of the second book of Chronicles and it is well worth recounting, as it is tells of a victory against overwhelming odds of the Southern Kingdom of Judah over the Northern Kingdom of Israel. Although the Bible does not tell us exactly when this battle took place, the fact that King Abijah only reigned for three years and the fact that the account of this battle is given immediately after the Bible informs us that Abijah had begun to reign, would seem to indicate that this battle took place very early in King Abijah's reign.

The account of the battle begins with informing us that there was war between King Abijah of the Southern Kingdom of Judah and King Jeroboam of the Northern Kingdom of Israel. These two kingdoms had been at war with each other for over seventeen years when Abijah became king of the Southern Kingdom of Judah and they remained at war with each other during his short three-year reign. It appears that one of the first things King Abijah did when he became king was to go out to battle against King Jeroboam with the purpose of winning back the Northern Kingdom of Israel to the Davidic Kingdom. He had an army comprising of four hundred thousand 'valiant men of war', whereas King Jeroboam had twice that number—eight hundred thousand 'chosen mighty warriors' (2 Chronicles 13:3). King Abijah was therefore outnumbered two to one, but this did not deter him. He and his army marched to Mount Zemaraim, which was situated in the highlands of Ephraim to the north of Jerusalem, and there he reminded King Jeroboam and his army that the Lord had given the kingship over Israel to David and his successors and reminded King Jeroboam of his rebellion and of his setting up in the Northern Kingdom of Israel the two golden calves that he had made as their gods. King Abijah also reminded him that he, King Jeroboam, had driven out those belonging to the Levitical Priesthood and had allowed anyone to purchase a priestly position for the price of a young bull or seven rams. He also accused King Jeroboam of forsaking the Lord. King Abijah then told King Jeroboam that the Lord was with him (King Abijah) and was at the head of his army and pleaded with King Jeroboam's army not to fight against the Lord because they would not succeed.

While this was going on, King Jeroboam had ordered some of his troops to go to the rear of King Abijah's army, so that King Abijah's troops were effectively surrounded by King Jeroboam's army, who were then lined up *in front of* and *behind* them. At this point, surrounded and outnumbered, King Abijah and his army cried out to the Lord, the priests who were with them blew their trumpets, and the army attacked King Jeroboam's army and defeated it, killing five hundred thousand of its eight hundred thousand soldiers. The Bible teaches quite clearly that King Abijah and his army achieved the victory because they relied on the Lord. King Abijah's army pursued the defeated army of King Jeroboam and managed to capture some of the cities, towns and villages that were located in the Northern Kingdom of Israel.

Although the record of King Abijah's reign in 1 Kings 15:3 is, as we have seen, quite disparaging, in 2 Chronicles 13:21 we are informed that King 'Abijah grew mighty'. The Bible then tells us that he took fourteen wives and had twenty-two sons and sixteen daughters. After this, we are told quite simply that he died (or 'slept with his fathers' as recorded in 2 Chronicles 14:1) and that he was buried in the city of David. Nothing else is recorded about King Abijah. We are not told how old he was when he became king or how old he was when he died and the Bible tells us nothing about what caused his death.

Jehoshaphat's father, Asa

King Abijah was succeeded by his son, Asa who reigned on the Throne of David for forty-one years from 910 BC to 869 BC. In 2 Chronicles 16:12, we are informed that, 'In the thirty-ninth year of his reign, Asa was diseased in his feet, and his disease became severe.' This would have been in 871 BC and because of this illness his son, Jehoshaphat, was actually co-regent with him for a period of three years, from 872 BC to 869 BC, at the beginning of his own twenty-four-year reign.

The Bible tells us that Asa was a good king (2 Chronicles 14:2) and proves this by informing us about some of the good things that he accomplished. After destroying the heathen altars and places where the people worshipped their false gods, King Asa commanded the people of the Southern Kingdom of Judah to keep God's laws and commandments. He built fortified cities that had towers and walls with strong lockable gates throughout the land. King Asa also built up a well-trained army of mighty men of valour, armed with bows and arrows, spears and large shields. With God's help, King Asa's army was able to thoroughly defeat an army of a million men and three hundred chariots (according to 2 Chronicles 14:9) led by Zerah, who is described as an Ethiopian. Celebrations for the victory of this battle took place in the 15th year of King Asa's reign—that is in 895 BC. Although there is no extra-biblical evidence regarding Zerah, it has been suggested that he was a general of the Egyptian army under the rule of Pharaoh Osorkon I, son of Shishak.[2] The Bible records that, as a result of the defeat of Zerah's army, King Asa's army chased them as far as Gerar in the southern coastal plain and then plundered the cities in that neighbourhood and also captured a great deal of livestock, including sheep and camels from the surrounding area. This would have greatly increased the prosperity of the Southern Kingdom of Judah.

King Asa used some of the treasure that he had taken from Gerar and the surrounding area in order to procure the help of Ben-hadad, King of Syria, in ending the invasion of the Southern Kingdom of Judah by King Baasha of the Northern Kingdom of Israel. According to an article in Wikipedia, these treasures, which King Asa took after he had defeated Zerah and his army, included 'the marvellous throne of Solomon upon which all the kings of Judah subsequently sat.'[3] The same article then goes on to point out that the treasures, given by King Asa to King Ben-hadad of Syria to obtain his alliance, were then taken 'by the Ammonites, to be recaptured by Jehoshaphat; then they fell into the hands of Sennacherib, from whom Hezekiah recovered them, and at the capture of Jerusalem they came into the hands of the Babylonians; then into those of the Persians, and afterward of the Macedonians, and finally of the Romans, who kept them at Rome.'[4]

After King Asa's victory over Zerah and his army, the Lord spoke to King Asa via the prophet Azariah and encouraged him to continue to serve the Lord. As a result, King Asa destroyed even more of the idols that were in the land and he also repaired the altar of the Lord that was in the courtyard of the Temple in Jerusalem. He even removed his grandmother, Maacah, from her position as the Queen Mother because she had erected an obscene idol of the fertility goddess, Asherah. King Asa had this idol cut down, chopped up and the pieces burnt in the Kidron Valley.

When people in the Northern Kingdom of Israel saw that God was with King Asa (2 Chronicles 15:9) and was blessing his kingdom, many of them, especially those from the tribes of Ephraim and Manasseh, began to move south to the Southern Kingdom of Judah. These people joined their fellow Israelites in Jerusalem to celebrate King Asa's victory of Zerah and his army. When King Baasha of the Northern Kingdom of Israel saw that some of his people were moving from his kingdom to King Asa's kingdom, he decided to try to stop this migration by fortifying the city of Ramah, which was located in the tribal area of Benjamin, and was about 5 miles (8 kilometres) north of Jerusalem. This occurred in the year 894 BC, a year after King Asa's victory over Zerah's army. An explanation of how this date has been computed is given in the notes and references at the end of this chapter.[5]

In order to stop King Baasha's fortification of the city of Ramah, King Asa took the silver and gold from the Temple in Jerusalem and from his own palace and sent them to Ben-hadad, King of Syria, in Damascus reminding him of the treaty that existed between King Asa's father (Abijah, aka Abijam) and King Ben-hadad's father (Tabrimmon), with the request that King Ben-hadad break his peace treaty with King Baasha and invade the Northern Kingdom of Israel. And this is what King Ben-hadad did—he sent his army into the Northern Kingdom of Israel and conquered the cities of Ijon, Dan,

Abel-maim (later known as Abel-beth-maacah) and all the store cities of Naphtali. As a result, King Baasha stopped building Ramah and hurried back home to Tirzah. King Asa then ordered his people to carry away the stones and the timbers that King Baasha had been using to build Ramah so that he could use them to fortify the cities of Geba and Mizpah in his own kingdom. The fact that King Asa relied on King Ben-hadad's help in forcing King Baasha to withdraw from his kingdom did not please the Lord and he sent Hanani, the seer, to inform King Asa of this. Hanani reminded King Asa that, when he had relied on the Lord, the Lord had given him a great victory over Zerah and his huge army, and he warned him that, because he had not relied on the Lord to defeat King Baasha, God would cause King Asa to have wars. This made King Asa so furious that he put Hanani in stocks in prison[6] and he also 'inflicted cruelties upon some of the people at the same time' (2 Chronicles 16:10).

The Bible tells us quite a lot about King Asa, King Jehoshaphat's father. However, although we know that King Asa's father was King Abijah (aka Abijam), the Bible does not tell us the name of his mother. We know that Maacah was his paternal grandmother and that she held the position of Queen Mother, until Asa removed her from this position because she had erected an obscene idol of the fertility goddess, Asherah. As with other kings, when King Asa obeyed the Lord's commandments, trusted the Lord in battle, and tried to please the Lord by cleansing the land of idols and the people of idol worship, the Lord blessed him and, as a result, the people who lived in his kingdom—the Southern Kingdom of Judah—were also blessed by God and became more prosperous. However, towards the end of his life, King Asa thought it better to trust people rather than the Lord. For example, he put his trust in King Ben-hadad of Syria when trying to stop King Baasha from fortifying the city of Ramah in order to prevent the migration of fellow Israelites from the Northern Kingdom of Israel into his Southern Kingdom of Judah. We know that this displeased the Lord and when God sent his messenger, Hanani, to tell King Asa, he was so annoyed that he imprisoned Hanani and put him in stocks. Also, during the last three years of his life, instead of seeking the Lord for the healing of his diseased feet, King Asa sought the help of physicians. Although we know that King Asa reigned for forty-one years from 910 BC to 869 BC, we do not know how old he was when he began to reign and, therefore, how old he was when he died. The Bible informs us that he was buried in the tomb that he had prepared for himself in the City of David.

Jehoshaphat's reforms

Jehoshaphat was thirty-five years old when he began to reign and he reigned for twenty-four actual years from 872 BC to 848 BC—the first three years were as co-regent with his father, King Asa, because of Asa's illness with his feet. For all his faults, King Asa was a good role model for Jehoshaphat and, as a result, King Jehoshaphat was a good king—the Bible telling us that he walked in the 'ways of his father David' (2 Chronicles 17:3). The first thing that Jehoshaphat did when he began to reign was to strengthen his kingdom against any attacks by the Northern Kingdom of Israel. He did this by stationing troops in his fortified cities and establishing garrisons in his kingdom and in the cities of Ephraim, which were in the Northern

Kingdom of Israel and which had been captured by his father King Asa. As a result, the kingdoms surrounding the Southern Kingdom of Judah ceased to make war with King Jehoshaphat and so began a time of peace between the Southern Kingdom of Judah and her neighbours. Furthermore, at this time the Philistines and the Arabians brought presents and gifts of silver and animals (rams and goats) to King Jehoshaphat, with the result that he and his kingdom steadily grew rich.

King Jehoshaphat then set about implementing religious and educational reform in his kingdom. He, himself, did not worship Baal, so he set about destroying the high places—that is the areas on the summits of the hills and mountains where the people worshipped Baal and committed idolatry.[7] He also destroyed the Asherah figures which were used in idol worship and exterminated the male cult prostitutes that remained from the time of his father, King Asa. In the third year of his reign—this would be when his father, King Asa, died (in 869 BC)—King Jehoshaphat sent officials and Levites around his kingdom to educate and teach the people the laws of God. He repeated this exercise some sixteen years later, after the death of King Ahab of the Northern Kingdom of Israel in 853 BC (see 2 Chronicles 19) but, this time, he appointed judges in his kingdom to judge impartially and without taking bribes over disputes and over cases 'concerning bloodshed, law or commandment, statutes or rules' (2 Chronicles 19:10).

Sometimes it is very difficult to work out when certain events that are recorded in the Old Testament actually occurred. Let us look at one classic example. We read in 2 Kings 19:35–37 that the angel of the Lord killed 185,000 Assyrian troops in their camp as they were preparing to attack the city of Jerusalem. We know that this event occurred in 701 BC and as a result, King Sennacherib of Assyria returned to Nineveh. The Bible actually records that he 'went home and lived at Nineveh. And as he was worshipping in the house of Nisroch his god, Adrammelech and Sharezer, his sons, struck him down with the sword and escaped into the land of Ararat. And Esarhaddon his son reigned in his place' (2 Kings 19:36–37). The impression given in the Biblical record is that these events happened almost one after another. But King Sennacherib was not assassinated by his two sons until the twentieth of the month of Teber (December/January) 681 BC,[8] some twenty years *after* he had returned from Jerusalem to live in Nineveh.

The relevance of telling this story is that there is an interesting piece of information about the life of Jehoshaphat in 1 Kings 22:47–49 which reads: 'There was no king in Edom; a deputy was king. Jehoshaphat made ships of Tarshish to go to Ophir for gold, but they did not go, for the ships were wrecked at Ezion-geber. Then Ahaziah the son of Ahab said to Jehoshaphat, "Let my servants go with your servants in the ships," but Jehoshaphat was not willing.' Then the Bible goes on to inform us that King Jehoshaphat died and was buried in the city of David. The three verses quoted above do not seem to belong here and seem completely out of place, coming, as they do, just before the account of King Jehoshaphat's death and burial. Actually, the Bible is recording events in King Jehoshaphat's life that do not come one after another but, as with the story of King Sennacherib, these events take place over a number of years. First of all, we are informed that there was no king in Edom and it is implicitly implied that King Jehoshaphat appointed one of his deputies as the ruler of Edom. Although we do not know *exactly* when this was, it would not have been until King Jehoshaphat established and strengthened his kingdom after the death of his father, King Asa, which occurred in 869 BC. The reference to King Jehoshaphat refusing King Ahaziah's request to allow his servants to go on King Jehoshaphat's ships[9] puts this event over a dozen years later in 853 or 852 BC, for these are the two years in which King Ahaziah reigned over the Northern Kingdom of Israel. Finally, the verse informing us about King Jehoshaphat's death and burial is recording an event that occurred four or five years later again in 848 BC. Hence, 1 Kings 22:47–50 actually covers a period of at least twenty-one years.

Jehoshaphat's friendship with King Ahab of the Northern Kingdom of Israel

King Ahab was married to Jezebel, daughter of Ethbaal, King of Sidon, and this marriage was probably arranged by Ahab's father King Omri in order to strengthen the relationship between the Northern Kingdom of Israel and the Kingdom of Phoenicia. As a daughter of a Phoenician king who was a high priest of the god Baal, Jezebel would probably have been a priestess of Phoenician deities, including Baal. King Ahab was influenced by his wife, Jezebel, for it appears that as soon as he married her, he began to worship Baal (1 Kings 16:31–32) and early in his reign, he built a temple in Baal's honour in the capital city of Samaria so that Baal could be worshipped there. Not only was an altar of Baal set up in the temple of Baal, but an Asherah pole was also erected in this temple (1 Kings 16:33). Now, as we have already noted, King Jehoshaphat did not worship Baal, yet incredibly he formed an alliance with King Ahab who was a celebrated and influential Baal worshipper.

We read in 2 Chronicles 18:1 that King Jehoshaphat made what is described as 'a marriage alliance with Ahab'. This would have been the arranged marriage of his eldest son, Jehoram (aka Joram), to King Ahab's daughter, Athaliah. At this time, the two Royal Houses of Judah and Israel tended to name their heirs after members of each other's Houses. As a result, Athaliah would have found it most confusing for she was married to Jehoram (aka Joram) and she had a brother who was named Joram (aka Jehoram). She and her husband Jehoram (aka Joram) had a son who they named Ahaziah, but he was also known as Jehoahaz *and* Azariah, which incidentally was also the name of another of Athaliah's brothers. Reading the relevant chapters about these people in the books of Kings and Chronicles can therefore be very confusing[10] especially as they all became monarchs of either the Southern Kingdom of Judah or the Northern Kingdom of Israel.

Now, not only did King Jehoshaphat form a marriage alliance with King Ahab, but he also joined him in a battle against the Syrians. When King Jehoshaphat was on a royal visit to the Northern Kingdom of Israel, King Ahab asked him to join with him in the battle to retake control of the city of Ramoth Gilead, which was within the territory of King Ahab's kingdom and which had been taken over by the Syrians. At King Jehoshaphat's insistence, the two Kings enquired of the Lord by assembling some four hundred prophets and asking them what they should do. With one exception, they all said that they should go into battle against the Syrians and that the Lord would give them the victory. However, through one of the Lord's prophets, Micaiah, the Lord said that King Ahab would die in battle if he went to war against the Syrians (2 Chronicles 18:4–27). However, they took no notice of Micaiah's prophecy and decide to go into battle against the Syrians and try to re-capture Ramoth Gilead. As they prepared for the battle, King Ahab suggested that King Jehoshaphat dress in his royal robes and that he, Ahab, would dress as an ordinary soldier. We can see clearly King Ahab hoped that, as a result of this, the Syrians would attack and kill King Jehoshaphat because he was dressed in his royal robes and that the Syrians would not attack King Ahab because he did not dress in his royal robes and looked like an ordinary soldier. But when the Syrian soldiers attacked King Jehoshaphat and heard him speaking, they realized that he was not King Ahab and so stopped attacking him. However, King Ahab was struck 'at random' according to the ESV translation—'by chance' according to the Good News Bible—by a Syrian's arrow between the joints in his armour and this caused him to collapse and bleed to death in his chariot—thus fulfilling the prophecy of Micaiah. King Jehoshaphat then returned to Jerusalem but, on the way, he was met by Jehu the Seer (that is, he was a prophet) who admonished him for helping the wicked and loving those who hate the Lord—an obvious reference to his alliance with King Ahab. He was, however, commended for destroying the Asherah figures in his kingdom and setting his heart to serve God.

There are often unforeseen consequences of choices that are made and one of the unforeseen consequences from King Jehoshaphat's decision of having a marriage alliance with King Ahab was that King Ahab's daughter, Athaliah, had a very evil influence over the monarchy of the Southern Kingdom of Judah. In the next paragraph, I shall attempt to give a brief history of the Southern Kingdom of Judah, from the death of King Jehoshaphat in 848 BC to the death of his great grandson King Joash in 796 BC—this is the time period which had disastrous consequences as a result of King Jehoshaphat's foolish alliance with the evil King Ahab of the Northern Kingdom of Israel. If the reader wishes to know more detail of the events that occurred during this period, then they can read about them in my other book about the lives and times of the kings in the Old Testament.[11]

Athaliah's evil influence on King Jehoshaphat's son, Jehoram (aka Joram), can be seen when King Jehoshaphat died and he became king. We read in 2 Chronicles chapter 21 that as soon as he became king and had established his throne, he killed his six brothers and also some of the princes of Israel. He did this so that there were no rivals to his being king. King Jehoram was an evil king who was influenced by his wife, Athaliah, who was the daughter of the wicked King Ahab. In addition to murdering his brothers, he re-established the high places in the hill country (these had been destroyed by his father, King Jehoshaphat, at the beginning of his reign) and he led the people of the Southern Kingdom of Judah into idolatry and apostasy. He reigned for seven actual years from 848 BC to 841 BC and he was so unpopular that when he died the Bible states that it was to 'no-one's regret' (2 Chronicles 21:20). When King Jehoram died, his youngest son, Ahaziah, became king because all his older brothers had been killed by 'the band of men that came with the Arabians to the camp' (2 Chronicles 22:1). He only reigned for part of the year 841 BC before he was killed by the newly appointed King Jehu of the Northern Kingdom of Israel. King Jehoram's widow,

Athaliah, then murdered all her grandchildren so she could be queen. However, one of her grandsons, Joash, was hidden in the Temple in Jerusalem for six years by his half-aunt, Jehosheba, who was Athaliah's half-sister, and who was married to Jehoiada, the priest. After six years, little six years old Joash was crowned king and his grandmother, Queen Athaliah, was executed. Joash reigned over the Southern Kingdom of Judah for thirty-nine actual years, from 835 BC to 796 BC. He ruled wisely while he was influenced and guided by his uncle, Jehoiada, but after he died, Joash turned his back on God and even had the prophet Zechariah[12] stoned to death when he rebuked him for forsaking the Lord. King Joash was eventually assassinated by two of his servants, who were eventually executed for this offence by Amaziah, Joash's son and successor, when he became king.

Jehoshaphat's unconventional battle plan

Earlier we looked at how, at the beginning of his reign, King Jehoshaphat implemented religious and educational reforms in his kingdom. We also saw that he reinforced these reforms later in his reign after the death of King Ahab of the Northern Kingdom of Israel in 853 BC but, this time, he also introduced judicial reforms by appointing judges in his kingdom to judge impartially and without taking bribes. After this, a coalition of Moabites, Ammonites and Meunites[13] assembled at Engedi, which lies on the mid-point of the western shore of the Dead Sea, ready to invade King Jehoshaphat's kingdom. When King Jehoshaphat was informed of this impending invasion, he was afraid and proclaimed a fast throughout his kingdom with the result that the people began to pray to the Lord for his help.

King Jehoshaphat himself went into the Temple at Jerusalem and he also prayed to the Lord for his help in this matter for, as he confessed in his prayer, he did not know what to do (2 Chronicles 20:12).

The people of the Southern Kingdom of Judah then assembled together in Jerusalem and the Lord answered the King's prayer by speaking to the people through the Levite, Jahaziel, when the Spirit of the Lord came upon him. Jahaziel told King Jehoshaphat and the people that they were not to be afraid or dismayed for, in that well-known and oft recited phrase, 'the battle is not yours but God's' (2 Chronicles 20:15). He then told the people that, on the next day, they were to go to where the enemy was—the Lord through Jahaziel even told them where the enemy was located—and they were told they did not need to fight the enemy but to stand firm and see the Lord win the victory for them. And this is what they did. The people of the Southern Kingdom of Judah set out early the next morning and went to where the Lord had told them the enemy would be—in the wilderness of Tekoa about 12 miles (19 kilometres) south of Jerusalem. King Jehoshaphat put his best singers, dressed in what the Bible states was 'holy attire' and he had these singers walk in front of his army singing:

> Give thanks to the Lord,
> for his steadfast love endures forever (2 Chronicles 20:21).

This refrain is similar to the first verse of both Psalm 106 *and* 107. When the Lord heard the praises of his people, the Lord caused panic in the enemy's army and this resulted in the Moabites and Ammonites turning on the Meunites and attacking them; when they had finished attacking and killing the Menuites, they began to attack and kill each other. King Jehoshaphat's army did not have to do any fighting at all, as he and his people saw when they entered the Wilderness of Tekoa and saw that all the soldiers of their enemy were dead. It took three days for King Jehoshaphat and the people to take all the 'goods, clothing and precious things' (v. 25) that were among the dead soldiers. They carried this spoil back to Jerusalem and went into the Temple and praised God with harps, lyres and trumpets. What a time of praise and worship that would have been! This story is an excellent illustration of a victory over the enemies of God's people by the Lord himself, with his people simply praying for his help, trusting in his word, worshipping him and then watching as God destroys his people's enemies and gives his people the victory.

Summary and conclusion

The Bible gives King Jehoshaphat a favourable obituary at the end of 2 Chronicles 20:32, where it tells us that he walked in the way of his father, Asa, and did not turn aside from doing what was right in the sight of the Lord. We have seen that his educational, religious and judicial reforms caused the people to learn the Law of the Lord and to follow the Lord. Yet, for all of King Jehoshaphat's reforms, not all the so-called *high places* were removed from his kingdom and people still made sacrifices and offerings at these locations. (1 Kings 22:43).

King Jehoshaphat was thirty-five years old when he began to reign and he reigned over the Southern Kingdom of Judah for twenty-five years, according to the Bible—this was twenty-four actual years. He therefore died when he was fifty-nine years old. His son Jehoram (aka Joram) reigned in his place and we have already seen what an evil, nasty king he turned out to be—a result of the marriage alliance that King Jehoshaphat made with King Ahab of the Northern Kingdom of Israel. The only other personal details that the Bible tells us about King Jehoshaphat (apart from the ones that we have looked at in this chapter) is that his mother's name was Azubah, the daughter of Shilhi, and that he was buried in the city of David.

NOTES

1 https://en.wikipedia.org/wiki/Death_and_taxes_(idiom)

2 John D. Currid, and David P. Barrett, *Crossway ESV Bible Atlas* (Wheaton, Illinois: Crossway, 2010), p. 150.

3 Article entitled 'Asa of Judah' in https://en.wikipedia.org/wiki/Asa_of_Judah

4 Ibid

5 In 2 Chronicles 16:1, we read that it was in the thirty-sixth year of the reign of King Asa that King Baasha invaded the Southern Kingdom of Judah and fortified the city of Ramah. Accepting this on face value, it is *impossible* for this to have happened as King Baasha would have been dead for ten years! The reference to the thirty-sixth year in this verse is actually a reference to its being the thirty-sixth year since the split of the United Kingdom of Israel in 930 BC—not to the thirty-sixth year of King Asa's reign. For those wanting a detailed explanation of this, see: Edwin R. Thiele, *The Mysterious Numbers of the Hebrew Kings, New Revised Ed.,* (Grand Rapids, MI: Kregel, 1983), p. 84.

6 King Asa seemed to have taken no notice of the stricture: "Don't shoot the messenger!"

7 This is why in the original Hebrew, Psalm 121:1 is in the form of the question 'Shall I lift up my eyes to the hills?' The answer, of course is 'No!' The Psalmist knew that looking to the tops of the hills and mountains for help was in fact looking to Baal or to other idols that were worshipped on the tops of the hills surrounding where you lived. The Psalmist then goes on to ask, 'From where does my help come?' and he answers, 'My help comes from the Lord who made heaven and earth.' Help does not come from Baal as the prophets of Baal learnt on Mount Carmel in Elijah's day, nor does it come from the idols that were worshipped on the hills and mountains.

8 Clive Anderson, *Sennacherib, Encountering Assyria's Great and Terrifying Ruler,* (Leominster: Day One Publications, 2007), p. 82.

9 More light is shed on this story in 2 Chronicles 20:35–37 where we read that King Jehoshaphat was condemned by the Lord via the prophet Eliezer for joining with King Ahaziah in building these ships so they could go to Tarshish. As a result, the Lord wrecked the ships that they had built and so Jehoshaphat's refusal to have any further contact or agreement with King Ahaziah can be fully understood.

10 To understand who's who and when they reigned and over which kingdom, it can be very useful to use the family tree in figure 3 on page 89 of my book *Rogues in Royal Robes*. (Leominster: Day One Publications, 2020).

11 See chapter 6 of *Rogues in Royal Robes,* pp. 103 onwards.

12 Zechariah was the son of Jehoiada and Jehosheba and so was Joash's half-cousin.

13 According to the footnote to 2 Chronicles 20:1 on page 767 in the *esv Study Bible* (Wheaton, Illinois: Crossway Bibles, 2008), the Meunites are equated with the people of Mount Seir on the southern border of Judah—this would accord with 2 Chronicles 20:22, where the coalition is listed as 'the men of Ammon, Moab, and Mount Seir'.

5 King Ahaz—faithless idolater

We saw in the last chapter that King Jehoshaphat of the Southern Kingdom of Judah died in 848 BC and that he was succeeded by his son Jehoram (aka Joram), who was married to Athaliah—the daughter of King Ahab of the Northern Kingdom of Israel. King Jehoram (aka Joram) reigned for seven years and was succeeded by his son Ahaziah, who reigned for part of the year 841 BC before he was assassinated by King Jehu of the Northern Kingdom of Israel. King Ahaziah's mother, Athaliah, then murdered her grandchildren so she could become the monarch. One grandson, Joash, escaped being killed by his grandmother for he was hidden in the Temple in Jerusalem by Athaliah's half-sister, Jehosheba, and her husband Jehoiada the Priest. Athaliah ruled for six years until her grandson, Joash was crowned king and she was executed. Joash had a long and a relatively trouble-free reign of thirty-nine years, from 835 BC to 796 BC until he was assassinated by two of his servants.

Now I want us to look at the main events that happened in the Southern Kingdom of Judah during the eighty-one-year period from the death of King Joash and the accession of his son Amaziah in 796 BC to the death of King Ahaz and the accession of his son, Hezekiah, in 715 BC. In addition to recounting the main happenings that occurred in the Southern Kingdom of Judah, we shall, from time to time, refer to some of the events that happened in the Northern Kingdom of Israel during this period—including its demise in 723 BC. There is a Chinese curse which says, 'May you live in interesting times.'[1] The period that we shall now look at in this chapter can certainly be called 'interesting times' and as the people turned their back on God and stopped worshipping and following him, they were certainly cursed.

King Amaziah

When King Joash was assassinated by two of his servants in 796 BC, he was succeeded by his son Amaziah. One of the first actions that King Amaziah took when he had firmly established himself as king was to execute the two servants who had assassinated his father, King Joash. He then led a campaign to gain control over Edom, which had been lost by King Jehoram (aka Joram) who was the son of King Jehoshaphat. Because the royal line in the Southern Kingdom of Judah was from father to son, King Jehoram (aka Joram) was actually King Amaziah's great grandfather. Being in control of Edom was important for King Amaziah since ruling that country meant being in charge of the southern trade routes in and out of the Southern Kingdom of Judah. King Amaziah hired a large contingent of soldiers from the Northern Kingdom of Israel (100,000 according to 2 Chronicles 25:6) to help him with his campaign. However, after advice from someone who is simply called 'a man of God' (2 Chronicles 25:7), King Amaziah dismissed these soldiers. These same troops took this as an insult and they vented their feelings by attacking and plundering various towns in the Southern Kingdom of Judah on their way back to their homes in the Northern Kingdom of Israel. According to 2 Chronicles 25:13, they struck down 3,000 people and took much spoil from the towns that they plundered.

King Amaziah was successful in conquering Edom and he

returned triumphant back to Jerusalem, bringing with him some of the gods of the people of Edom. What happened next is mindboggling and defies any rational explanation in view of King Amaziah's obedience to the Lord's instructions so far in his reign. King Amaziah set up these idols as his own gods and bowed down to them and burned sacrifices to them! Needless to say, the Lord was very angry with King Amaziah's worshipping and making sacrifices to these false gods and so he sent a prophet (we do not know his name because the Bible does not give it) to speak to him about this. However, the King refused to listen to him and interrupted what he had to say, warning the prophet that if he did not stop speaking, he would have him struck down. The prophet did stop speaking but not before telling King Amaziah that God had decided to destroy him because of what he had done and also because he had not listened to what he, the prophet, was saying.

However, elated by his victory over Edom, King Amaziah then plotted against the Northern Kingdom of Israel and sent a message to King Jehoash (aka Joash)[2] of the Northern Kingdom of Israel, challenging him to a battle. He responded by suggesting that King Amaziah should give his daughter in marriage to King Jehoash's son and advised King Amaziah to stay at home! King Amaziah, however, refused to listen to King Jehoash and went to war against him at Beth-shemesh,[3] and King Amaziah's army was defeated. King Jehoash took King Amaziah prisoner and, first of all, he was taken to Jerusalem where King Jehoash's army tore down about 600 feet (about 180 metres) of the city walls. King Jehoash's troops then looted the gold and the silver and the palace articles that were in the Temple and took them, together with King Amaziah and hostages, back to their own capital city, Samaria, in the Northern Kingdom of Israel, where King Amaziah was imprisoned. Now, one of the problems we have in following the story of what happened after King Amaziah was taken captive to Samaria is that the accounts written in 2 Kings 14:17–22 and 2 Chronicles 25:23–28 and 26:1–3 are *not* written chronologically. This has been ably demonstrated by Professor Thiele, who has managed to work out the correct chronological sequence for what happened at this time.[4]

As an aside, although no archaeological finds relating directly to King Amaziah have been discovered, a reference to a contemporary of his—King Jehoash of the Northern Kingdom of Israel—has been found.[5] On a stela, discovered in 1967 by the British archaeologist, the late Professor David Oates at Tell al Rimah—which is about 50 miles (80 kilometres) west of Mosul in Iraq—there are twenty-one lines of text referring to a campaign of the Assyrian King, Adad-nirari III, in the Mediterranean area. On this stela, there is mention of the receipt of tribute paid by King Jehoash of the Northern Kingdom of Israel in 796 BC. This was two years after Jehoash became king of the Northern Kingdom of Israel and the year that King Joash of the Southern Kingdom of Judah was assassinated and his son Amaziah became king. This is, again, proof that the kings who are mentioned in the Bible were real people and were not mythical monarchs as they were once thought to be.

Now to get back to our story about the kings who reigned on the Throne of David over the Southern Kingdom of Judah. As soon as King Amaziah was taken captive to Samaria by King Jehoash, the people in the Southern Kingdom of Judah appointed King Amaziah's son, Uzziah (aka Azariah) as their king. You might get the impression from reading the Bible that this event happened *after* King Amaziah was released from prison in Samaria, but actually, it was *before*. King Amaziah remained in prison in Samaria until the death of King Jehoash of the Northern Kingdom of Israel in 782 BC. He was then released and returned to the Southern Kingdom of Judah, where he lived in Lachish for the next fifteen years. Because of opposition to his being king, (remember his son, Uzziah [aka Azariah] was reigning as king at this time), he did not occupy his throne in Jerusalem, but fled to the town of Lachish which is some 30 miles (40 kilometres) southwest of Jerusalem. King Amaziah was eventually assassinated there in 767 BC and his body was returned on horseback to Jerusalem where he was buried in the royal tombs of David's City.

The Bible informs us in 2 Chronicles 25:1 that Amaziah reigned for twenty-nine years in Jerusalem. As we saw in the previous paragraph, this is not literally true although it can be argued that he was king over the Southern Kingdom of Judah for all of this time— even though he did not rule over his kingdom for all of this time. He started his reign in 796 BC and, after his defeat by King Jehoash of the Northern Kingdom of Israel at the battle at Beth-shemesh, he was taken prisoner and was incarcerated in the capital city, Samaria, for ten years until the death of King Jehoash in 782 BC. He then returned to the Southern Kingdom of Judah and lived in the town of Lachish, until he was assassinated fifteen years later in 767 BC— some twenty-nine years after he began to reign in 796 BC.

King Uzziah (aka Azariah)

King Amaziah's son, Uzziah (aka Azariah), was only sixteen years old when he began to reign over the Southern Kingdom of Judah instead of his father, Amaziah, who had been taken prisoner and was now languishing in prison in Samaria, the capital of the Northern Kingdom of Israel. King Uzziah had a long reign—fifty-two years from 792 BC to 740 BC, the first twenty-five years of which overlapped with his father Amaziah. At the beginning of his reign, advised and guided by Zechariah,[6] King Uzziah obeyed God and the Lord prospered him. The first thing that Uzziah did when he became king was to invade and defeat the Philistines and the Arabians. He then fortified Jerusalem with towers and built fortified cities in the territories of the defeated Philistines and Arabians, as well as in other strategic locations in his own kingdom. The Bible informs us that, such was his fame that even the Ammonites paid tribute to him. King Uzziah reorganised his army and strengthened it by supplying it with 'shields, spears, helmets, coats of mail, bows, and stones for slinging' (2 Chronicles 26:14). Skilful members of his army constructed war machines which could be positioned on the towers of Jerusalem and which could be used to shoot arrows and catapult huge stones at any attackers. King Uzziah was not only interested in warfare, but he was also interested in agriculture and, as a result of his interest in soil, he knew its fertility and therefore knew where to locate his farmers, herdsmen and vinedressers. He also had wells dug so that his people's cattle and crops would be well-watered.

But, after he had been reigning for forty-two years, King Uzziah made the same mistake as King Saul made in that he took no notice of God's commandments regarding the law that only Levites could make offerings to the Lord—in Saul's case, it was a burnt offering; in Uzziah's case, it was incense. King Uzziah entered the Temple in

Jerusalem in order to burn incense on the altar. However, Azariah, the chief priest, with eighty other priests went in after him and told him that what he was about to do was wrong, for only the priests who were the sons of Aaron were consecrated and therefore allowed to burn incense. The King took no notice of them and became very angry and had the censer in his hand ready to offer the burnt incense when suddenly leprosy appeared on his forehead. As a result, King Uzziah was rushed out of the Temple and, because he was a leper, he had to live in a separate house for the rest of his life. This occurred in the year 750 BC and, because of King Uzziah's leprosy and his being prohibited from meeting with his officials, Uzziah's son, Jotham was made co-regent with his father until his father died ten years later in 740 BC at the age of sixty-eight. The year in which King Uzziah died (740 BC) was also the year when the prophet Isaiah had his vision of 'the Lord sitting upon a throne, high and lifted up; and the train of his robe filled the temple' (Isaiah 6:1).[7] Because the year when Jotham became co-regent with his father was reckoned as Jotham's official first year, the sixteen official years of Jotham's reign recorded in 2 Chronicles 27:1 are in fact fifteen actual years.

Total eclipse of the sun on 15 June 763 BC

Before we look at what happened during the reign of King Jotham, I want us to look at one very important event that happened during the reign of King Uzziah—one that is not recorded in the Bible, but one which has a profound effect on our understanding of *when* events which are recorded in the historical books of the Old Testament occurred. This event is the spectacular total eclipse of the sun that occurred on 15 June 763 BC. The date of this eclipse has been established not only by astronomical computations but also by observations that are recorded in Assyrian records. Obviously, the people living in Assyria at the time did not refer to the year as 763 BC because, as correctly pointed out by two curators of the British Museum, 'nobody knew they were BC. There was no epoch-making moment from which each year was counted. One system gave names to each year. The king and his counsellors would discuss the significant events of the past year'[8] and as a result of their deliberations, they would choose one (usually a person) to be commemorated and so, the next year would be known by the name of this eponym. This spectacular solar eclipse took place in the month that the Assyrians called *Simanu* (that was the third month covering parts of our May and June) in the year of the eponym, *Bur-Sagale*, during the 10th year of the reign of Ashur-dan III, King of Assyria. Astronomical computations have shown that this was on 15 June 763 BC and I have deliberately referred to it as being 'spectacular' because totality would have been seen from the northern part of the Philippines; through south west China; through what is now north Pakistan; through the countries on both sides of the Caspian Sea; through what is now Turkey and the eastern part of the Mediterranean Sea; through what is now Libya and the Sahara Desert; and finishing on west coast of Africa.[9] People living in the Middle East could not miss this solar eclipse as the totality was over the northern part of the Assyrian Empire and the inhabitants of countries such as Israel would have seen a partial eclipse.

So, how does this solar eclipse help us with our understanding of *when* events which are recorded in the historical books of Old

Testament occurred? Using this 'fixed' date of 15 June 763 BC and the Assyrian eponym lists, Professor Edwin Thiele has shown that, in 853 BC, King Shalmaneser III of Assyria fought a coalition of a dozen kings, including King Ahab of the Northern Kingdom of Israel, at the battle of Qarqar—an ancient town on the banks of the Orontes River in north-western Syria.[10] He has also shown that twelve years later, in 841 BC, King Shalmaneser III of Assyria received tribute from King Jehu of the Northern Kingdom of Israel. From this data and information given in the Bible, Professor Thiele has shown that King Ahab of the Northern Kingdom of Israel died in 853 BC and Jehu acceded to the throne of the Northern Kingdom of Israel in 841 BC. Thus, we have a definite link between the chronology of the Northern Kingdom of Israel which is found in the Bible and the absolute chronology of Assyria. Now the dates of the reign of King Tiglath-Pileser III of Assyria have also been fully established from the date of this eclipse. Both the Bible and the Assyrian records report King Menahem, King Pekah and King Hoshea of the Northern Kingdom of Israel and King Uzziah and King Ahaz of the Southern Kingdom of Judah had dealings with King Tiglath-Pileser III, showing that the Biblical chronologies are entirely consistent with the Assyrian chronology—which is accepted without doubt by the academics who study the history of Assyria. Furthermore, Professor Edwin Thiele has also established another chronological link between the Bible and the absolute chronology of the Assyrian empire from the eponym list—from this he has determined that King Sennacherib of Assyria invaded the Southern Kingdom of Judah at the time of King Hezekiah in 701 BC. All these chronological links, calculations and interlocking of dates are basically the result of determining the date of this spectacular solar eclipse on 15 June 763 BC!

King Jotham

As we have seen, Jotham became co-regent with his father, King Uzziah for ten years—from 750 BC to 740 BC —when Uzziah was stuck with leprosy while he was attempting to burn incense in the Temple. The reason that the Lord struck him down was because King Uzziah was of the tribe of Judah and only those descended from Aaron of the tribe of Levi were permitted to burn incense as an offering in the Temple. We have also seen that Jotham reigned as king of the Southern Kingdom of Judah for fifteen actual years—from 750 BC to 735 BC. He was therefore the sole ruler for only five years—from 740 BC to 735 BC. However, King Jotham did not die until 732 BC so, for the period 735 BC to 732 BC, there was an overlap with his son Ahaz—but this was *not* a co-regency. To appreciate this, we must note that, in the annals of Tiglath-Pileser III, we learn King Uzziah was a prominent anti-Assyrian ruler in the countries in the western part of the Assyrian Empire. King Uzziah's son, Jotham, was also anti-Assyrian but Jotham's son, Ahaz, was not and, as a result, Ahaz was put on the throne by the pro-Assyrian faction in his kingdom in 735 BC, some three years before his father, King Jotham, died in 732 BC. However, Ahaz was firmly in control during these three years—his father King Jotham playing no part in ruling his kingdom. This is re-enforced by the fact that these three years are not included in calculating the number of years that King Jotham reigned because, in 2 Chronicles 27:8, we read that he reigned for sixteen years—that is fifteen actual years; this would be from 750 BC to 735 BC—even though he did not die until 732 BC. But neither are these three years included when the length of the reign of King Ahaz is given in 2 Chronicles 28:1, for here we are informed that King Ahaz reigned for sixteen years. However, we know that King Hezekiah (King Ahaz's son) began his reign in 715 BC because it is recorded in Isaiah 36:1 that, in the fourteenth year of his reign, King Sennacherib of Assyria invaded the Southern Kingdom of Judah—this was in 701 BC, a date which is firmly established in the Assyrian chronology. Therefore, it can be argued that King Ahaz reigned for twenty years from 735 BC to 715 BC. Such an anomaly as these 'three missing years', if the reason behind it is not fully understood, can often cause confusion in determining when kings reigned and when events actually happened.

The following is a summary of the reigns and the pertinent events that happened during the reigns of the kings of the Southern Kingdom of Judah that are discussed in the above paragraphs and will, I am sure, help the reader to follow more closely what happened.

DATE(S)	KING AND PERTINENT EVENT OF HIS REIGN
750 BC–740 BC	Jotham co-regent with his father Uzziah
750 BC–735 BC	Jotham reigned over the Southern Kingdom of Judah
740 BC–735 BC	Jotham sole ruler over the Southern Kingdom of Judah
735 BC	Ahaz elected king over the Southern Kingdom of Judah by pro-Assyrian faction

735 BC–732 BC	Ahaz ruled over the Southern Kingdom of Judah while his father King Jotham was still alive
735 BC–732 BC	These three years are not included (that is, counted) in either King Jotham's reign in 2 Chronicles 27:1 or in King Ahaz's reign in 2 Chronicles 28:1
732 BC	Jotham died
735 BC–715 BC	Total reign of Ahaz (but as already stated, the first three years are excluded in 2 Chronicles 28:1)
723 BC	Fall of city of Samaria and demise of the Northern Kingdom of Israel
715 BC	Ahaz died and his son Hezekiah began to reign
701 BC	14th year of Hezekiah's reign
701 BC	Sennacherib, King of Assyria invaded the Southern Kingdom of Judah

King Jotham was King Hezekiah's grandfather and he was twenty-five years old when he began to reign in 750 BC—hence he would have been forty-three years old when he died in 732 BC. The Bible informs us that he did right in the eyes of the Lord (2 Chronicles 27:2) but then goes on to inform us in the same verse that he did not enter the Temple (these days, this is the equivalent of not going to church). However, he had the North Gate of the Temple rebuilt and he had extensive work carried out on the city wall in the area of Jerusalem called Ophel, which is on the eastern ridge and descends south of the Temple.[11] King Jotham also fortified his realm by building cities in the hill country and forts and towers on the wooded hills of his kingdom. The Bible informs us that during the five years that King Jotham was the sole ruler of the Southern Kingdom of Judah—that is from 740 BC to 735 BC—he fought against and defeated the Ammonites and they paid a considerable tribute to him for a period of three years (2 Chronicles 27:5). This three-year period was probably from 738 BC to 735 BC. However, the Ammonites stopped paying this tribute when Jotham's son, Ahaz, succeeded him.

Under King Jotham's reign, the people of his kingdom followed what are described as 'corrupt practices' (2 Chronicles 27:2). These 'corrupt practices' refer to the fact that the people sacrificed and made offerings on the high places which King Jotham had not removed (2 Kings 15:35). Isaiah, who ministered at the time that Jotham reigned, drew attention to the wickedness of the people of the Southern Kingdom of Judah in Isaiah 1 and, in Isaiah 2:8, he drew attention to the fact that the land was full of idols and the people were bowing down to these idols that they had crafted with their own hands and fingers. Furthermore, in chapter 3 of the prophetic book bearing his name, Isaiah describes the latest clothing, jewellery and fashion accessories of the women who lived in Jerusalem at the time and warned them that the Lord would judge them for their silly behaviour and obsession with fashion. In addition, Isaiah warned the men that they would also be judged and, as a result, they would be killed in battle. This is what happened some 150 years later, when the Babylonian army invaded the Southern Kingdom of Judah and eventually destroyed Jerusalem in 586 BC.

King Ahaz

Sometimes it is easy to forget the relationship of one king to another as we look at the different kings that occupied the Throne of David. In this section, I want us to look at the life of King Ahaz, who was the son of King Jotham. King Ahaz was a really nasty piece of work in that he did not follow the Lord and was utterly idolatrous. We have already seen that he took over the throne of his father, Jotham, and, although he did not kill his father, it is obvious that he did not allow him to rule, as was his right. King Ahaz did not worship the Lord, but he 'sacrificed and made offerings on the high places and on the hills and under every green tree' (2 Chronicles 28:4). In other words, he worshipped Baal and Asherah and, as recorded in 2 Chronicles 28:3, he even worshipped Molech (the evil Canaanite god of the Ammonites) for he sacrificed his sons by burning them as offerings in the Valley of Hinnom.[12] As a result of King Ahaz's idolatry, the Lord caused the Southern Kingdom of Judah to be attacked from all quarters—the northeast, the north, the southeast and the southwest, in that order.

First of all, King Ahaz's kingdom was attacked from the northeast and it was defeated by Syria, who took people from the Southern Kingdom of Judah captive back to their capital Damascus. Then, the Northern Kingdom of Israel, under the leadership of King Pekah, invaded the land from the north and again the Southern Kingdom of Judah was defeated. According to 2 Chronicles 28, 120,000 'men of valor (sic)' were killed (v.6), and 200,000 relatives and 'much spoil' were taken back to Samaria, the capital of the Northern Kingdom of Israel (v.8). However, when the army together with their captives and the spoil arrived at Samaria, they were met by Oded, a prophet of the Lord, who was supported by leaders of the tribe of Ephraim. Oded admonished the army and reminded them that the Lord was angry with the Southern Kingdom of Judah and, as a result, the Lord had given them into the hand of the army of the Northern Kingdom of Israel. Oded then told the army that the rage with which they had killed and defeated the Southern Kingdom of Judah had reached heaven. He reminded the army that, although their intention was to enslave all those they had captured, they had ignored their own sin. Oded then instructed the army to return all the captives back to their own land. To facilitate this, the leaders of the tribe of Ephraim fed and clothed the captives and helped them to return home with all the spoil that had been taken from their kingdom.

Now, while this was going on, King Ahaz appealed to Tiglath-Pileser III, King of Assyria for help because the Southern Kingdom of Judah had been invaded from the southeast by the kingdom of Edom and from the southwest by the Philistines. However, Tiglath-Pileser III did not help him but took advantage of his weakened position, with the result that King Ahaz paid him tribute in order to placate him. This probably took place in the year 732 BC, which was towards the beginning of King Ahaz's reign.[13] James Bennett Pritchard (1909–1991) was an eminent Biblical archaeologist at the University of Pennsylvania and he edited a classical anthology of the ancient Near East which is often cited as *ANET* – the full title of which is *Ancient Near East Texts Relating to the Old Testament*. According to an article in this anthology, the name of Ahaz is included in a list of rulers in the Mediterranean area who paid tribute to King Tiglath-Pileser III.[14] This, again, shows that the kings mentioned in the historical books in the Old Testament were real people and events in their lives are not only recorded in the Bible but also, as in the case of King Ahaz, in the annals of the kings of Assyria.

Northern Kingdom of Israel during the reign of King Ahaz

We noted, in chapter three, that the monarchal line in the Northern Kingdom of Israel was not from father to son, as it was in the Southern Kingdom of Judah, but was overturned by assassinations, murders, court plots and even a suicide! To appreciate the state that the Southern Kingdom of Judah was in when King Ahaz died and his son Hezekiah became king in 715 BC, we have to understand what had been happening in Northern Kingdom of Israel. To do this, we have to go back almost forty years to the year 753 BC—that is three years *before* King Uzziah (aka Azariah) of the Southern Kingdom of Judah was struck down with leprosy. In that year, Zechariah succeeded his father King Jeroboam II as king of the Northern Kingdom of Israel. He had only reigned in Samaria for six months when Shallum, of whom we know nothing except that we are informed he was the son of Jabesh,[15] assassinated King Zechariah and reigned in place of him. But King Shallum had reigned for only one month when another usurper, Menahem, attacked Samaria from Tirzah, where he was based at the time, and murdered King Shallum and reigned instead of him. King Menahem was a very cruel king—we are informed in 2 Kings 15:18 that he did what was evil in the sight of the Lord and that he did not depart from the sins of Jeroboam II. To give one example of how this wicked king behaved, it is recorded, in 2 Kings 15:16, that he attacked Tiphsah[16] and, because its citizens did not surrender to him, he had all the pregnant women 'ripped open' and all its inhabitants killed. King Menahem reigned from his palace in Samaria over the Northern Kingdom of Israel for ten years from 752 BC to 742 BC and he was succeeded by his son, Pekahiah, who ruled for two years from 742 BC to 740 BC.

But, to fully understand and appreciate what was happening in the Northern Kingdom of Israel during the reigns of King Menahem and his son King Pekahiah, we must go back to 752 BC when Menahem murdered King Shallum and began to reign from his palace in Samaria. At the same time Pekah, of whom we know nothing except that he was the son of Remaliah, set himself up as a rival king—his reign overlapping for ten years with King Menahem and then for two years with Menahem's son, King Pekahiah, whom Pekah assassinated in 740 BC. In 2 Kings 15:25, we are informed that this assassination took place 'in Samaria, in the citadel of the King's house with Argob and Arieh'. There has been much discussion and also some disagreement between scholars, translators and commentators about the exact meaning of these two words—some think that they are the result of scribal errors; some consider that they are place names; while others maintain they are the names of people. However, when comparing these two words with the Ugaritic[17], it would appear that they mean 'eagle' and 'lion', respectively, and that they actually refer to the guardian sphinxes which were engraved on ivory plaques and erected in the gateway of the King's palace.[18]

Although we cannot be one hundred percent certain, it would appear that, when Pekah set up his rival kingdom in 752 BC, he probably located his capital in Gilead, as this would help explain the following three puzzling points, we come across in the historical books of the Bible that cover the period from 752 BC to 723 BC:

- The ambiguity of whether the father of King Shallum (who Menahem murdered so he could be king) was from Jabesh *in* Gilead or whether his father was Jabesh *of* Gilead—this ambiguity has already been pointed out in note 14 of the endnotes of this chapter.
- If Pekah ruled his rival kingdom from Gilead, it would explain why Pekah was helped by 'fifty men of the people of Gilead' (2 Kings 15:25), when he assassinated King Pekahiah in 740 BC so that he could become the king of the Northern Kingdom of Israel.
- Although the relevant passages in the historical books of the Bible do not explicitly state the existence of two rival kingdoms in the Northern Kingdom of Israel at this time, their existence can be inferred from the prophecy of Hosea (which was written at the time), for, in Hosea 5:5, 'Israel' and 'Ephraim' are not synonymous but are referred to as two separate entities in the original Hebrew.[19]

At the time that Pekah assassinated King Pekahiah in 740 BC, the Bible described Pekah as a captain of King Pekahiah (2 Kings 15:25). From this, it looks as if Pekah (who had set up a rival kingdom to King Menahem, the father of King Pekahiah) had developed a friendship with King Pekahiah and eventually occupied a prominent military position in his army while plotting to acquire the whole of the Northern Kingdom of Israel. After Pekah had assassinated King Pekahiah, he then ruled as the sole monarch of the Northern Kingdom of Israel from its capital Samaria for the next eight years, until he himself was assassinated in 732 BC by Hoshea, who was a captain in his army. It would appear that Hoshea had placed himself at the head of the pro-Assyrian faction in the Northern Kingdom of Israel and, as a result of his assassinating King Pekah, King Tiglath-Pileser III of Assyria rewarded him by making him king of the Northern Kingdom of Israel. This is confirmed on an undated inscription of Tiglath-Pileser III where he boasts of making Hoshea king after his predecessor had been overthrown:

> Israel (literally "Omri-house" *Bit-Humria*) ... overthrew their king Pekah (*Pa-qa-ha*) and I placed Hoshea (*A-ú-si'*) as king over them. I received from them 10 talents of gold, 1,000(?) talents of silver as their [tri]bute and brought them to Assyria.[20]

Although the amount of tribute exacted from King Hoshea by Tiglath-Pileser III is not specifically stated in the Bible, we do know that King Menahem paid 1,000 talents (about 33.5 tons or 34,000 kilograms) of silver[21] to King Tiglath-Pileser III about ten years previously to 'help him to confirm his hold on the royal power' (2 Kings 15:19)—ironically this was against King Menahem's rival, Pekah.

King Hoshea ruled for the next nine years—from 732 BC until 723 BC—and he continued to pay tribute to Assyria, first to King Tiglath-Pileser III and then to his successor, his son King Shalmaneser V. When King Hoshea stopped paying tribute to the Assyrians and, because he had made contact with So, King of Egypt (2 Kings 17:4),[22] King Shalmaneser V imprisoned Hoshea, invaded the Northern Kingdom of Israel and besieged its capital Samaria for three years until it fell in 723 BC.[23] This marked the end of the Northern Kingdom of Israel—the inhabitants of the kingdom and of its capital Samaria were taken captive by the Assyrians and, according to 2 Kings 17:6, they were taken to three areas in the Assyrian Empire:

- Halah—in spite of much speculation, no one really knows *exactly* where this was,
- Habor/Gozan—the Khabur River, a tributary that flows south into the River Euphrates from the highlands of south-eastern Turkey and north-eastern Syria, and
- the Cities of the Medes—south-western Iran.

The Bible informs us that this occurred because the people had sinned against the Lord their God and had served other gods. Furthermore, the Lord had sent prophets to warn them what would happen to them if they did not heed God's warnings, but they had not listened and had continued to follow their own ungodly ways and worship the idols that they made. As a result of their being defeated and being taken into captivity by the Assyrians, the people of the Northern Kingdom of Israel effectively disappeared from history.

The dates given in the preceding paragraphs for the reigns of the kings who ruled over the Northern Kingdom of Israel from 753 BC to 723 BC are taken from Professor Edwin Thiele's book, *The Mysterious Numbers of the Hebrew Kings*. In this book, Professor Thiele convincingly shows that Pekah set up a rival kingdom during the reigns of King Menahem and his son King Pekahiah.[24] He also deals with the apparent logistical problems that arise with what is written in 2 Kings 17:1 about when King Hoshea began to reign over the Northern Kingdom of Israel and in 2 Kings 18:1 about when King Hezekiah began to reign over the Southern Kingdom of Judah.[25]

Summary and conclusion

In this chapter, we have looked at the lives of the kings who reigned over the Southern Kingdom of Judah from the time that King Jehoshaphat died in 848 BC to the time that King Ahaz died in 715 BC—a period of 133 years. At one point in this chapter, we reminded ourselves of the Chinese curse which says, 'May you live in interesting times.' The 133-year period, that we have considered, can certainly be labelled 'interesting times' and as the kings turned their back on God and stopped worshipping and following Him, they and the people they reigned over were certainly cursed—especially those in the Northern Kingdom of Israel which ceased to exist in 723 BC.

King Jehoshaphat was succeeded by his son Jehoram (aka Joram), who was married to Athaliah, the daughter of the wicked King Ahab of the Northern Kingdom of Israel. King Jehoram (aka Joram) was not a good king; he reigned for seven years and when he died, in 841 BC, the Bible records that it was to no one's regret. He was succeeded by his son, Ahaziah, who reigned for only a part of the year 841 BC before he was assassinated by King Jehu of the Northern Kingdom of Israel. King Ahaziah's mother, Athaliah, then murdered her grandchildren so that she could become the monarch and she ruled for six years until her grandson, Joash, who had been hidden in the Temple in Jerusalem by Athaliah's half-sister, Jehosheba, and her husband Jehoiada the Priest, was crowned king and Athaliah was executed. King Joash reigned for thirty-nine years, from 835 BC to 796 BC, and was a good king while he was being advised by his uncle, Jehoiada the Priest, but as soon as his uncle died, he turned away from the Lord and even oversaw the execution of his half-cousin Zechariah, who warned him to forsake his wicked ways.

King Joash was assassinated by two of his servants and he was succeeded by his son, Amaziah, who, after he had executed these two servants, led a campaign against Edom to gain control over the southern trade routes in and out of his kingdom—trade routes that had been lost by King Jehoram (aka Joram), the son of King Jehoshaphat. King Amaziah returned triumphant back to Jerusalem, bringing with him some of the gods of the people of Edom which he set up as his own gods and worshipped and burned sacrifices to them. This caused the Lord to be very angry and He sent an unnamed prophet to inform King Amaziah that God had decided to destroy him because of what he had done. King Amaziah thought that nothing could destroy him and he went to war against King Jehoash of the Northern Kingdom of Israel. His army was defeated and King Amaziah was taken captive and imprisoned in King Jehoash's capital city, Samaria, until King Jehoash died in 782 BC. He was then released and returned to the Southern Kingdom of Judah, where he lived in Lachish until he was assassinated fifteen years later.

As soon as King Amaziah was taken captive to Samaria by King Jehoash, the people in the Southern Kingdom of Judah appointed his son, Uzziah (aka Azariah) as their king. King Uzziah was a good king who was interested in both warfare and agriculture. At the beginning of his reign, he invaded and defeated the Philistines and the Arabians. He then fortified Jerusalem with towers and built fortified cities in the territories of the defeated Philistines and Arabians, as well as in other strategic locations in his own kingdom. King Uzziah reorganised his army and strengthened it by supplying it with materials that were used for both defence and assault purposes. Skilful members of his army also constructed war machines. King Uzziah had a love of agriculture and he was so interested in the fertility of soil that he knew where to locate his farmers, herdsmen and vinedressers. He also had wells dug so that his people's cattle and crops would be well-watered. However, after he had been reigning for forty-two years, King Uzziah made the same mistake as King Saul made in that he took no notice of God's commandment that only Levites could make offerings to the Lord—in Saul's case, it was a burnt offering; in Uzziah's case, it was incense. As a result of his attempting to offer incense in the Temple, leprosy suddenly appeared on King Uzziah's forehead. King Uzziah was rushed out of the Temple and, because he was a leper, he had to live in a separate house for the rest of his life. Due to King Uzziah's leprosy and his being prohibited from meeting with his officials, Uzziah's son, Jotham was made co-regent with his father until Uzziah died ten years later, in 740 BC, at the age of sixty-eight.

To fully understand the history of the Southern Kingdom of Judah from the time King Jotham became co-regent (with his leprous father, King Uzziah) in 750 BC to when his son King Ahaz died in 715 BC, we have to try to understand the political leanings of the kings at the time—especially those in the Northern Kingdom of Israel where there was a kingdom within the kingdom being ruled by a different king from the king who was ruling the main kingdom! It is not just the case of who was ruling when (and where), but whether he was pro- or anti-Assyria. The history was also muddied by the Assyrians themselves making alliances with the kingdoms that surrounded the land of Israel. During the reigns of Jotham and

Ahaz, there were actually four kings of the Northern Kingdom of Israel. One of these, King Pekah, reigned in Gilead at the same time as King Menahem and his successor—his son King Pekahiah— reigned from Samaria. King Pekah assassinated King Pekahiah in 740 BC and was then the sole ruler of the whole of the Northern Kingdom of Israel until 732 BC when he was assassinated by Hoshea—who was then appointed king by Tiglath-Pileser III, King of Assyria. When King Hoshea rebelled against Assyria and stopped paying tribute, the Assyrians invaded his kingdom, destroyed its cities, including its capital Samaria, and took the inhabitants of the Northern Kingdom of Israel captive, removing them to distant parts of the Assyrian Empire. This captivity had been foretold in the Law and by the prophets, who the Lord sent to warn the people of the error of their ways. The people and their rulers would not listen to the Lord and so the Northern Kingdom of Israel ceased to exist.

We also saw in this chapter that Assyrian records document a spectacular solar eclipse which took place in the month that the Assyrians called Simanu (that was the third month covering parts of our May and June) in the year of the eponym, *Bur-Sagale*, during the 10th year of the reign of Ashur-dan III, King of Assyria. Astronomical computations have shown that this was on 15 June 763 BC and, as a result of this 'fixed date', scholars have been able to determine exactly *when* events which are recorded in the historical books of Old Testament occurred. For example, the dates of the reign of King Tiglath-Pileser III of Assyria have been fully established from the date of this eclipse and both the Bible and the Assyrian records report that King Uzziah and King Ahaz of the Southern Kingdom of Judah and King Menahem, King Pekah and King Hoshea of the

Northern Kingdom of Israel had dealings with King Tiglath-Pileser III. We therefore have definite links between the chronology of the Southern Kingdom of Judah and the Northern Kingdom of Israel, which are found in the Bible, and the absolute chronology of Assyria. Such chronological links are basically the result of determining the date of this spectacular solar eclipse on 15 June 763 BC! And these links show that the kings that we read about in the Bible ruling over the Southern Kingdom of Judah and the Northern Kingdom of Israel were not mythological monarchs but were real royals who lived in genuine palaces which were located in actual cities in real kingdoms.

NOTES

1 https://en.wikipedia.org/wiki/May_you_live_in_interesting_times
2 King Jehoash of the Northern Kingdom was also called Joash and this can cause a little confusion because King Amaziah's father was also called Joash as well as Jehoash! Joash is the shortened form of Jehoash and both names mean the same: *Jah supports*. For clarity, I have used the name Jeohash for the name of the king of the Northern Kingdom of Israel and Joash for the name of the king of the Southern Kingdom of Judah. For those who are interested, the king of the Northern Kingdom of Israel is called Joash in 2 Kings 13:9, 12, 13 and 14, and in 14:1 as well as in 2 Chronicles 25:17, 18, 21, 23 & 25. However, he is called Jehoash in 2 Kings 13:10 and in 14:8, 9, 11, 13, 15, 16, 17 & 23. And in 2 Kings 13:25, he is called by *both* names in the *same* verse!
3 Beth-shemesh is a small town about 19 miles (30 kilometres) west of Jerusalem in the Sorek Valley on the northern border of the Southern Kingdom of Judah.
4 Edwin R. Thiele, *The Mysterious Numbers of the Hebrew Kings: New Revised Edition,* (Grand Rapids, MI: Kregel, 1983), pp. 113–116.
5 https://watchjerusalem.co.il/665-tell-al-rimah-stele-king-jehoash-found
6 This was *not* Zechariah, the son of King Jeroboam II who reigned over the Northern Kingdom of Israel for six months nearly forty years later in 753 BC. Nor was he Zechariah, the prophet, who wrote the book bearing his name that we find in the Bible, for he lived almost three hundred years after King Uzziah.
7 Isaiah was the son of Amos and according to rabbinic tradition, Amos was King Amaziah's

brother. If this is so, Isaiah would have been a member of the Royal Family of the Southern Kingdom of Judah. See https://en.wikipedia.org/wiki/Amaziah_of_Judah

8 Irving Finkel, and Jonathan Taylor, *Cuneiform*, (London: The British Museum, 2015), p. 90.

9 https://eclipse.gsfc.nasa.gov/SEatlas/SEatlas-1/SEatlas-0779.GIF

10 Edwin R. Thiele, *The Mysterious Numbers of the Hebrew Kings*, pp. 112–113.

11 https://en.wikipedia.org/wiki/Ophel#Meaning_of_the_term

12 This is from where we get the word *gehenna*—meaning hell.

13 Edwin R. Thiele, *The Mysterious Numbers of the Hebrew Kings*, p. 133.

14 James B. Pritchard, (Editor), *Ancient Near East Texts Relating to the Old Testament [2nd edition]*, (Princeton University Press, 1955), p. 282.

15 As Edwin Thiele has pointed out on page 124 of his book, *The Mysterious Numbers of the Hebrew Kings*, this could also indicate that Shallum was from Jabesh in Gilead rather than that his father's name was Jabesh. Edwin Thiele then points out that this would help to explain the support that King Pekah received from 'fifty men of Gilead' in his overthrow of King Pekahiah, son and successor of King Menahem, who had assassinated King Shallum and taken his throne.

16 According to https://www.bible-history.com/schaffs/t/tiphsah/ this place is one of several places:
   (i) A city on the western bank of the Euphrates, which is represented in Greek and Latin by Thapsacus, a town situated at one of the most frequented fords of the Euphrates
   (ii) A town in Palestine, near to Tirzah
   (iii) What is now an unknown ford of the River Jordan
   (iv) The ruin Tafsak, south of Shechem.

17 'Ugaritic' is an extinct Northwest Semitic language classified by some as a dialect of the Amorite Language. https://en.wikipedia.org/wiki/Ugaritic

18 *Baker Encyclopedia of the Bible*, [1997 edition]: Entry for *Pekah* (volume 4, p. 1636).

19 See section: C. Lederer, and H.J. Cook, *A Rival Reign in Gilead* in https://en.wikipedia.org/wiki/Pekah

20 https://en.wikipedia.org/wiki/Hoshea

21 That is about twenty-one and a half million pounds' worth of silver in today's money (as of November 2020).

22 The footnote on 2 Kings 17:3–4 in the *esv Study Bible* (Wheaton, Illinois: Crossway Bibles, 2008), states: 'The identity of "So, King of Egypt" is a matter of debate. The pharaoh in question might have been Osorkon IV, the last pharaoh of the 22nd dynasty (730 BC–715 BC) or Tefnakht, founder of the overlapping and rising 24th dynasty (727 BC–720 BC). Some scholars have proposed an Egyptian military commander named Sib'e, but he is unknown in any other texts. Alternatively, "So" may not be a personal name but may be based on the

name of the town, "Sais", the capital of King Tefnakht.'

23 The Bible tells us in 2 Kings 17:5 that King Shalmaneser V invaded the Northern Kingdom of Israel and besieged the city of Samaria for three years before it fell. Professor Edwin Thiele has shown (in his book: *The Mysterious Numbers of the Hebrew Kings,* on pp. 137–138 & 163–172) that the first destruction of Samaria by the Assyrians took place in 723 BC during the reign of Shalmaneser V who reigned from 727 BC to 722 BC. But Sargon II, who reigned from 722 BC to 705 BC, claimed that he took Samaria and, as a result, 722 BC came to be looked upon as the date of Samaria's fall. This date is found in almost all commentaries, encyclopaedias and textbooks that record the date of the fall of Samaria. Professor Thiele has pointed out that a number of outstanding scholars have carefully studied this subject and all have definitely concluded that Samaria fell in 723 BC and this is the date that I have consistently used in this book.

24 Edwin R. Thiele, *The Mysterious Numbers of the Hebrew Kings,* pp. 124–131.

25 Ibid, pp. 134–138, 174–175.

6 King Hezekiah – faithful and good

One of the main purposes of my writing about the kings that we find ruling over the Northern Kingdom of Israel and the Southern Kingdom of Judah in the Old Testament is to show that they were not figments of the imaginations of the people who wrote about them, but they were real people. They were not mythological monarchs ruling over magic kingdoms but were real royals who lived in real palaces which were in real cities and that they ruled over real people who lived in real kingdoms. They were kings of flesh and blood—cut them and they bled as we do. Even though they lived over two and a half thousand years ago, they experienced the whole gamut of human emotions as we do, living in the 21st century—including ambition, anger, covetousness, disappointment, forgiveness, greed, grief, happiness, hatred, hunger, impatience, jealousy, joy, loneliness, love, lust, pleasure, sorrow, temptation, thirst, tiredness, and weariness. And just as we do, they experienced aches and pains, illness and even death itself. These kings that we read about in the Old Testament craved power and authority, as well as success, many possessions, immense wealth and numerous women. King Hezekiah's life reflected that he experienced many of these emotions and ambitions and we know this because he is mentioned not only in the Bible, but also in the Assyrian historical records. This king was no mere mythical monarch—he was a genuine king who was the ruler of the Southern Kingdom of Judah for twenty-nine years, from 715 BC to 686 BC. According to the Bible: 'He did what was right in the eyes of the Lord, according to all that David his father had done' (2 Kings 18:3). In other words, he was a good and faithful king, as we shall see.

King Sargon II of Assyria

We saw in the last chapter that Hoshea, the last king of the Northern Kingdom of Israel, rebelled against the Assyrians who were instrumental in putting him on the throne and, as a result, King Shalmaneser V of Assyria imprisoned King Hoshea, invaded his kingdom and besieged its capital Samaria for three years until it fell in 723 BC. Shalmaneser's successor was his brother, Sargon II, another son of Tiglath-Pileser III. Sargon II, who reigned over Assyria from 722 BC to 705 BC, was one of the most important kings of the Assyrian Empire and was the founder of the Sargonid Dynasty, which ruled Assyria for the next century until its collapse between 612 BC and 609 BC. The family tree of the Sargonid Dynasty is given on page 129 and this shows the relationships of the Assyrian kings to each other. Sargon II is known as 'a great military leader, tactician, patron of the arts and culture, and a prolific builder of monuments, temples, and even a city. His greatest building project was the city of Dur-Sharrukin ("Fortress of Sargon", modern day Khorsabad, Iraq) which became the capital of the Assyrian Empire under his reign.'[1]

Incredibly, until the middle of the 19th century no reference to King Sargon II had been found in any Assyrian records that had been discovered up to that time. The only reference to this most important king of the Assyrian Empire was in the Bible—in Isaiah

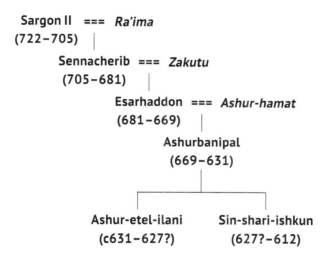

THE FAMILY TREE OF THE SARGONID DYNASTY

The names in italics are wives or concubines.

All the dates are BC and are the actual dates that the monarchs reigned.

In Ezra 4:10, King Ashurbanipal is called Asnappar in the King James Version and Osnappar in the English Standard Version of the Bible.

Sargon II === *Ra'ima*
(722–705)

    Sennacherib === *Zakutu*
    (705–681)

        Esarhaddon === *Ashur-hamat*
        (681–669)

            Ashurbanipal
            (669–631)

Ashur-etel-ilani   **Sin-shari-ishkun**
(c631–627?)   (627?–612)

20:1. And, typical of the way that so-called scholars view the Bible, it was concluded that King Sargon II had never existed and that he was some mythical monarch made up by the prophet Isaiah. But he did exist, as archaeologists found out when, in 1843, the great city of Dur-Sharrukin, which had been built by King Sargon II, was discovered on the banks of the Tigris River about 9.5 miles (15 kilometres) north-east of Mosul in Iraq. In this city, the archaeologists discovered that the city and palace gateways were guarded by huge five-legged, human-headed, winged bulls standing about 15 feet (4.5 metres) high and weighing about 10 tons.[2] King Sargon's great palace had two hundred and forty rooms, most of which were decorated with stone slabs that depicted military campaigns, the punishments of rebels, banqueting feasts and sporting activities. Narratives of the events, depicted on these reliefs, were also carved into these stone slabs.

The reference to King Sargon II in Isaiah 20:1 refers to the fact that the Assyrian army attacked the Philistine city of Ashdod and captured it. The footnote in the ESV *Study Bible* on Isaiah 20:1[3] gives us more information about this campaign which took place in 712/711 BC and is documented in the annals of King Sargon II, which have been found in Dur-Sharrukin and which confirm that King Sargon II sent a military commander to capture Ashdod, while he remained in the capital city that he was building. Interestingly, archaeologists have discovered fragments of an inscribed pillar of King Sargon II at Ashdod and this is a duplicate of a victory pillar found at Dur-Sharrukin. Furthermore, about three thousand human skeletons have been found at Ashdod and it is thought that these are the remains of the people that died as a result of the Assyrian capture of that city.

The question that needs answering is this: Why did no-one know about Dur-Sharrukin and King Sargon's palace? To understand the answer to this question, we must look briefly at the life of King Sargon II and appreciate his relationship with his son and successor, Sennacherib. King Sargon II began to build the city of Dur-Sharrukin in 713 BC after he had been reigning nine years. It would appear that he took a personal interest in every aspect of the city's construction, as his official letters, which were found in the archives of Kalhu and Nineveh, make clear. However, from time to time, so that he could deal with any rebellions and uprisings that occurred in various parts of his Empire, King Sargon II had to leave the building of Dur-Sharrukin and consign the administration of his Empire to the capable hands of his son, Sennacherib. It was while quelling a rebellion in Tabal, a province in central Anatolia, that King Sargon II met his death in 704 BC. Apparently, the people in Tabal had broken away from the Assyrian Empire and King Sargon II needed to bring the region back into the Empire. By this time, the building of the new capital city of Dur-Sharrukin was complete and the King felt comfortable in leaving Sennacherib in charge of the government of his Empire as he led his army across Mesopotamia and into Anatolia. The forces that had been assembled in Tabal put up a strong opposition to the Assyrian army and King Sargon II was killed in the fighting. The battle was so severe that the King's body could not be recovered from the battlefield and so was lost to the enemy. As a result, the Assyrians were driven from Tabal. They returned home without the body of their king and this was interpreted as an evil omen—that the gods had abandoned King Sargon II.

In his article about King Sargon II, Professor Joshua Mark writes that, as a result of King Sargon's humiliating defeat in Tabal, coupled with his death and the fact that the Assyrians could not bring the King's body back from the battlefield, 'Dur-Sharrukin was abandoned immediately and the capital moved to Nineveh by Sargon's successor, Sennacherib. The new King, who had been repeatedly left at home while Sargon II embarked on glorious campaigns, clearly resented his father as he wrote nothing and built nothing to honor (sic) his memory. None of Sennacherib's inscriptions mention his father at all and no building or monument was raised in his name.'⁴ As time went on, the Assyrians gradually forgot that Sargon had ever reigned or even existed. The city of Dur-Sharrukin with its magnificent city and palace gateways which were guarded by huge human-headed, winged bulls, its 240-roomed palace with all its reliefs and paintings stood empty, as everything which could be moved had been taken to Nineveh. Gradually the city, together with its palace, was covered by the sand and dust, and the knowledge of its existence, together with that of King Sargon II who built it, faded.

Ironically, the city of Nineveh—the city that Sennacherib, the son of Sargon II, established as the capital of the Assyrian Empire—suffered a similar fate to that of Dur-Sharrukin. King Sennacherib made Nineveh a truly magnificent city covering almost 1800 acres and having fifteen great gates in its walls. An elaborate system of eighteen canals supplied water from the hills to its 100,000 to 150,000 inhabitants (that is more than twice as many as lived in the city of Babylon at the time). The foundation of the King's palace was made up of about *160 million* bricks. It had eighty rooms and the stone carvings on the walls included battle scenes, impaling of captives and scenes showing Sennacherib's troops parading the spoils of war before him. As in Dur-Sharrukin, the principal doorways were flanked by colossal stone, human-headed, winged bulls. Some scholars have suggested that the gardens which Sennacherib built next to his palace, with its associated irrigation works, were the original 'Hanging Gardens of Babylon'. The city of Nineveh was destroyed by the Babylonians in August 612 BC when King Sin-shar-ishkun, who was King Sennacherib's great-grandson, was killed. The prophet Nahum had warned the Assyrians that their capital would be burned (Nahum 3:1–3 & 15), and this is how the Babylonians destroyed Nineveh. Gradually the city was covered over with sand, as predicted in Zephaniah 2:13, and, just like Dur-Sharrukin, it seemed that Nineveh had never existed. When the Greek historian, Xenophon[5], visited the site of Nineveh in the 4th century BC, he described it as 'abandoned' and, even though its location was known to some throughout the Middle Ages, it was not until 1847 that Austen Henry Layard discovered its palace with its literally miles of wall reliefs, some of which are now in the British Museum in London. If you look carefully (as I have done) at these reliefs, you can see clearly that some of them are fire-blackened which shows just how accurate Nahum's prophecy proved to be.

Hezekiah's religious reforms

It was in the year 715 BC, when twenty-five-year-old Hezekiah became king of the Southern Kingdom of Judah. From this information, we can calculate that Hezekiah was born in 740 BC. From information given elsewhere in the Bible we can calculate that his father, Ahaz, was only twelve years old when Hezekiah was born.[6] When Hezekiah became king, the Northern Kingdom of Israel no longer existed—it had ceased to exist eight years previously (in 723 BC) when the Assyrian army led by King Shalmaneser V had destroyed its capital Samaria and began deporting its inhabitants. As we have seen, Shalmaneser's successor was his brother, Sargon II, another son of Tiglath-Pileser III. He began to reign in 722 BC and he continued the policy of deporting the inhabitants of the Northern Kingdom of Israel into areas of the Assyrian Empire, which were literally hundreds of miles away. We know this because, in his annals, Sargon II claimed:

> At the beginning of my royal rule, I ... the town of the Samarians I besieged, conquered (2 lines destroyed) [for the god ...] who let me achieve this my triumph ... I led away as prisoners [27,290 inhabitants of it (and) equipped from among them (soldiers to man)] 50 chariots for my royal corps ... The town I rebuilt better than it was before and settled therein people from countries which I had conquered. I placed an officer of mine as governor over them and imposed upon them tribute as is customary for Assyrian citizens.[7]

As I have shown in my other book about the kings in the Old Testament,[8] the deportations by the Assyrians of the Israelites from the area of the Northern Kingdom of Israel and their replacement with peoples from other areas of the Assyrian Empire, gave rise to the Samaritans who we read about in the New Testament.

In spite of what was happening to his fellow Israelites in the Northern Kingdom of Israel, King Ahaz, Hezekiah's father, became less and less faithful to the Lord—see 2 Kings 16:10–20 and 2 Chronicles 28:22–27. He did not worship or serve the Lord but he dismantled and cut up the vessels that were used in the Temple for worshipping the Lord and then he shut up the doors of the Temple for two reasons according to Josephus[9]:

- to prevent the priests from entering the Temple in order to carry out the ritual sacrifices, and
- to cover up the King's stealing of the gifts that the people had placed in the Temple.

King Ahaz not only made altars in every corner of Jerusalem, but he also constructed so-called 'high places' in every city in the land so that sacrifices to other gods could be made. Furthermore, he sacrificed to the gods of Damascus. King Ahaz eventually died in 715 BC and the Bible records that he was not brought 'into the tombs of the kings of Israel' (2 Chronicles 28:27).

When Hezekiah inherited the throne[10] and became the king of the Southern Kingdom of Israel, things did not look good. The Northern Kingdom of Israel no longer existed—its capital had been destroyed some eight years previously by the Assyrian arm-flung corners of the Assyrian Empire under the new ruler of Assyria—Sargon II, who was Shalmaneser's brother. As a result of the faithlessness of King Ahaz— Hezekiah's father—Hezekiah could not be certain whether the people of the Southern Kingdom of Judah would turn back to the Lord. But King Hezekiah was a man of faith and, as soon as he ascended the throne, he set about reversing the ungodly practices introduced by his father. First of all, *in the very first month of his reign*, he set about opening up and cleansing the Temple—he got the doors repaired and had all the rubbish that had accumulated in the Temple completely removed and then, with the aid of the priests, he had the Temple consecrated and the people cleansed by sacrificing seven bulls, seven rams, seven lambs and seven male goats. The sacrificing of the animals was accompanied by much singing, which in turn was accompanied with musical instruments. The Bible tells us that the people 'sang praises with gladness, and they bowed down and worshipped' (2 Chronicles 29:30), and after this time of praise and worship, the people brought in their own sacrifices and thank offerings. There were so many animals brought to be sacrificed— seventy bulls, one hundred rams, two hundred lambs for the burnt offerings and six hundred bulls and three thousand sheep for the consecrated offerings—that there were not enough consecrated priests to cope with their slaughtering. They had to consecrate some more priests and they also had to get their fellow Levites to help.

King Hezekiah then decided that the Passover should be celebrated in the second month of his reign and he sent invitations to the children of Israel to attend this Passover via letters, which he sent not only to the people dwelling in his own kingdom—the Southern Kingdom of Judah—but to everyone living in land of Israel, from Beersheba to Dan.[11] The Bible informs us that not everyone in the former territory of the Northern Kingdom of Israel accepted this invitation and the couriers of the invitations were sometimes 'laughed them to scorn and mocked them' (2 Chronicles 30:10). However, some people from the tribes of Asher, Ephraim, Issachar, Manasseh and Zebulun (2 Chronicles 30:11,18) did accept the invitation and went to Jerusalem to keep this Passover. We are informed that a very great assembly took part in this Passover and, afterwards, the people who had taken part helped to destroy the numerous idols, including the bronze serpent that Moses had made,[12] the Asherah poles, the high places and the pagan altars that were in the Southern Kingdom of Judah, before they returned to their homes.

Speaking about King Hezekiah, 2 Kings 18:7 informs us that 'the Lord was with him; wherever he went out, he prospered.' Verses such as this one are often used to re-enforce the erroneous view believed by some Christians that, if you follow God (as King Hezekiah did), the Lord will keep you from being attacked by your enemies, give you health so that you will never be sick and also ensure you live until you are very old. Such a view is not Biblical and one that certainly did not apply to King Hezekiah, as we shall see.

Hezekiah's life in chronological order

One of the problems we face when we read about the lives of the kings in the books of Kings and Chronicles is that often the accounts of their lives are not written in the chronological order in which they occurred—and this is certainly true in the case of King Hezekiah. Firstly, we will look at the chronological order of the life of King Hezekiah as recorded in 2 Kings and then as revealed in 2 Chronicles. Finally, we will look at the correct chronological order of his life.

In 2 Kings 18, we are informed that Hezekiah ascended the throne when he was twenty-five years old and that 'he removed the high places, and broke the pillars and cut down the Asherah' (v. 4a). Then, in v. 4b, there is an account of his destroying the bronze serpent that Moses had made. After this, we are informed that he rebelled against the Assyrians and struck down the Philistines 'as far as Gaza' (v. 8). Most of the rest of chapter 18 and all of chapter 19 records the account of the invasion of the Southern Kingdom of Judah by the Assyrians and how the Lord destroyed the Assyrian army. In chapter 20, we are informed about King Hezekiah's illness and how the Lord healed him and, as a result, he then received letters and a present from envoys from the King of Babylon. At the end of chapter 20, there is a short note about the pool and conduit that King Hezekiah constructed in order to bring water into the city of Jerusalem.

In 2 Chronicles, the story of King Hezekiah is told in a slightly different order. In chapter 29, we are again informed that Hezekiah was twenty-five years old when he began to reign. Then we are told the story of how the first thing that King Hezekiah did was to cleanse the Temple and celebrate the Passover, to which he invited the children of Israel from his own Southern Kingdom of Judah and from the recently defeated Northern Kingdom of Israel—we looked at this in detail above. However, this is omitted from the account of King Hezekiah's reign that is recorded in 2 Kings, where we are given the impression that the first thing he did, was to remove the high places, break the pillars and cut down the Asherah poles. In 2 Chronicles, we are informed that this occurred *after* the celebration of the Passover (2 Chronicles 31:1), but this celebration is not mentioned at all in 2 Kings. In 2 Chronicles we are told that King Hezekiah organised the re-introduction of Temple worship by putting the Levites and priests back into their holy offices and ensured that they were properly cared for (2 Chronicles 31:2-21). Again, this is not recorded in 2 Kings. The story of the Assyrian invasion, the Lord's destruction of the Assyrian army, Hezekiah's illness, the visit of the Babylonian envoys, and the diversion and construction of the water supply to Jerusalem is very similar to that which is recorded in 2 Kings. However, these events did *not* occur in this order as we shall see.

To sort out the real chronological order of the life of King Hezekiah, we have to start with his death which occurred in 686 BC. When he was ill, God healed him and through the prophet Isaiah promised him fifteen more years of life. We can therefore calculate that his illness and his healing would have happened in 701 BC, the same year that King Sennacherib invaded the Southern Kingdom of Judah—the fourteenth year of King Hezekiah's reign according to 2 Kings 18:13. King Hezekiah's illness and subsequent healing would have taken place at the beginning of the year because we are informed, in 2 Samuel 11:1, that kings go off to war in the spring. As pointed out by Clive Anderson in his book about King Sennacherib:

> Winter with its harsh weather would not have been conducive to marching out, so it was spent preparing for any forthcoming campaign, and that is what Sennacherib did in the winter of 702–701 BC.[13]

News of King Hezekiah's illness and recovery reached Merodach-baladan, the son of Baladan, King of Babylon and he sent envoys with letters and a present to King Hezekiah. This is recorded in 2 Kings 20:12 and in Isaiah 39:1 and briefly mentioned in 2 Chronicles 32:31, where it is recorded as having taken place *after* the invasion of the Southern Kingdom of Judah by the Assyrians. However, this visit took place immediately after Hezekiah's healing and therefore it must have occurred *before* King Sennacherib's invasion of the Southern Kingdom of Judah. Merodach-baladan was actually a king in exile at this time for he had lost his throne to Assyria a few years before.[14] However, he was openly active against Assyria and it can be argued that King Sennacherib heard about this visit and thought that King Hezekiah was trying to form an alliance with Babylon in order to strengthen his kingdom against any Assyrian attack. This would have incensed King Sennacherib and made him all the more determined to invade and conquer King Hezekiah's Southern Kingdom of Judah.

We saw in chapter 4 of this book, when we were considering the life of King Jehoshaphat, that sometimes it is very difficult to work out when certain events that are recorded in the Old Testament actually occurred. The Bible records that, after the destruction of

Jerusalem, the Assyrian King, Sennacherib, 'went home and lived at Nineveh. And as he was worshipping in the house of Nisroch his god, Adrammelech and Sharezer, his sons, struck him down with the sword and escaped into the land of Ararat. And Esarhaddon his son reigned in his place' (2 Kings 19:36–37). The impression given in the Biblical record is that these events happened almost one after another. But King Sennacherib was not assassinated by his two sons until 681 BC, some twenty years *after* he had returned from Jerusalem to live in Nineveh.

From the details about the life of King Hezekiah that I have outlined in the paragraphs above, we are able to determine that the true chronology for King Hezekiah is as follows:

- King Hezekiah inherited the throne from his father, King Ahaz, in 715 BC at the age of twenty-five.
- The Temple was cleansed and a Passover was celebrated immediately (that is, in 715 BC) for the children of Israel from both the Southern Kingdom of Judah and the recently defeated Northern Kingdom of Israel.
- Immediately after the celebration of the Passover, all the high places as well as the pagan pillars and altars and Asherah poles were destroyed together with the bronze serpent that Moses had made.
- Temple worship was then re-introduced.
- King Hezekiah then rebelled against the Assyrians and struck down the Philistines as far as Gaza.
- King Hezekiah's illness and healing occurred at the beginning of 701 BC.
- Envoys brought a present from Merodach-baladan, the King

of Babylon in exile, for King Hezekiah when they visited him after his healing in early 701 BC.

- The Southern Kingdom of Judah was invaded by the Assyrians in spring 701 BC and the Lord destroyed the Assyrian army.
- King Hezekiah died in 686 BC at the age of fifty-four.
- King Sennacherib was assassinated by his sons in 681 BC.

The construction of King Hezekiah's tunnel, and the dates when its excavation was carried out, will be considered in the next section.

Hezekiah's tunnel

At the end of the accounts of the life of King Hezekiah in both 2 Kings 20:20 and 2 Chronicles 32:30, it informs us that King Hezekiah constructed a conduit and brought water into Jerusalem. Why did he do this and when? The answers to these questions are tied up with the death of King Sargon II of Assyria who, as we saw earlier in this chapter, died in 705 BC. This would have been when King Hezekiah rebelled against the King of Assyria (2 Kings 18:7)—this was presumably King Sennacherib, the son and successor of King Sargon II. Afraid that King Sennacherib would invade his kingdom, which he did four years later, King Hezekiah made sure that the Assyrians did not have access to fresh water, when they invaded, by stopping the flow of water from all the springs in the land. He also diverted the upper outlet of the Gihon Spring and channelled the water down to the west of the City of David (2 Chronicles 32:30). This civil engineering project included the construction of what has come to be known as 'Hezekiah's Tunnel' under Jerusalem. This tunnel is about a third of a mile (1,749 feet or 533 metres) long and has an average gradient of 0.6% as it only falls about one foot (30cms) from one end of the tunnel to the other. It was not constructed in a straight line but was S-shaped, as can be seen in the map reproduced on page 143.[15] The reason for this is that the tunnellers probably followed a naturally occurring underground stream or karstic channel,[16] as this would explain how the tunnel was built so quickly (in under four years) and how the two groups of tunnellers, starting from opposite ends, were able to construct the tunnel with such accuracy that they met each other at a halfway point. The tunnel ran from the Gihon Spring near the floor of the Kidron Valley, which is outside the eastern wall of Jerusalem and wound underground (160 feet [49 metres] below the surface at its deepest point) to the Siloam Pool, which is well within the city walls.

We know that the tunnellers met at a half-way point because they chiselled into the rock where they met an inscription, which was discovered in 1880 by a young boy who was playing in the tunnel. The Siloam Inscription, as it is called, was subsequently chiselled out (causing some damage to it) and it is now in the Istanbul Archaeological Museum. An English translation of the six lines of Old Hebrew inscription reads:

1. [...] the tunnelling. And this is the narrative of the tunnelling: While [the stonecutters were wielding]
2. the picks, each toward his co-worker, the picks, each toward his co-worker, and while there were still three cubits to tunnel through, the voice of a man was heard calling out
3. to his co-worker, because there was a fissure in the rock, running from south [to north]. And on the (final) day of
4. tunnelling, each of the stonecutters was striking (the stone) forcefully so as to meet his co-worker, pick after pick. And

5. then the water began to flow from the source to the pool, a distance of 1200 cubits. And 100

6. cubits was the height of the rock above the head of the stone-cutters.[17]

Hezekiah and the Assyrian wolf

I have taken the title of this section from the opening stanza of Lord Byron's famous poem, 'The Destruction of Sennacherib'[18], which echoes the havoc that the Assyrian 'wolf' had wreaked upon the countries that surrounded the Southern Kingdom of Judah in the 8th century BC:

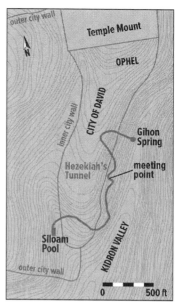

Map showing the path of Hezekiah's Tunnel

The Assyrian came down like the wolf on the fold,
And his cohorts were gleaming in purple and gold;
And the sheen of their spears was like stars on the sea,
When the blue wave rolls nightly on deep Galilee.

The invasion of the Southern Kingdom of Judah by the Assyrians in 701 BC must have brought terror into the hearts of its inhabitants, for it was less than a generation since the Assyrians had invaded the Northern Kingdom of Israel and had destroyed its capital. Now the Assyrians were invading the Southern Kingdom of Judah and were attacking and capturing all the fortified towns and cities—just as they had done in the Northern Kingdom of Israel before attacking and destroying its capital, Samaria, twenty-two years previously in 723 BC.

King Sennacherib and his army eventually reached Lachish which, after Jerusalem, was the second most important city of the kingdom and which was located about 30 miles (48 kilometres) southwest of Jerusalem. King Hezekiah begged King Sennacherib for a peace treaty and, as a result, King Hezekiah gave King Sennacherib 'all the silver that was found in the house of the Lord and in the treasuries of the King's house' (2 Kings 18:15). From the weight of the gold and silver given in 2 Kings 18:14, this was equivalent to almost fifty-seven million pounds in today's money. A cynic may point out that the Assyrians were charging the Israelites to live in the land that God had given them! But King Hezekiah had every reason to be afraid of the invading Assyrian army and tried to negotiate a peace treaty in order to prevent the Assyrians from attacking and destroying Jerusalem, for history illustrated that the Assyrians were masters of siege warfare and no city or fortress could stand before their assault.

The Assyrian army was composed of well-trained soldiers who were well-equipped and who were led by brilliant generals. The army was composed of chariots, cavalry and infantry and it also used effective siege engines and battering rams to break down walls over which its troops, using ladders, could then climb and enter the besieged town or city. The chariots used by the Assyrian army had a solid platform on which there were two soldiers: one controlled the two or three horses that pulled it; the other fought the enemy using a bow and arrows. The platform of the chariot was supported by two, sometimes four, wheels that had metal tyres made of copper, bronze or iron. The Assyrian cavalrymen wore light armour and carried weapons such as five-foot-long, metal-pointed, wooden spears, javelins and daggers as well as bows and arrows with iron heads. The infantry was composed of soldiers armed with shields, swords, spears, javelins, daggers, bows and arrows, and slings. These slings were not children's slings but were ones that could project smooth stones the size of tennis balls at 100–150 mph (about 160–250 kph) and could seriously injure or kill anyone that was hit by such a missile. The siege engines consisted of a tank-like wooden structure which ran along on four or six wheels. On top of this was a small wooden tower on which archers provided covering fire as the whole machine was pushed forward, usually up an earth ramp that had been built by the Assyrian troops and which reached right up to the walls that were to be attacked. The archers on the siege engine, together with the whole structure, were kept doused with water in order to extinguish any flaming torches thrown by the enemy from the tops of the walls that were under attack. A very large, long log with a metal tip was then placed at the front of this formidable siege engine with which to attack the walls of the town or city that was being besieged.

The savagery and brutality displayed by the Assyrian army knew no bounds. The leaders of the enemy were usually publicly humiliated in victory parades before being disembowelled, skinned alive, impaled on stakes, or mutilated in one way or another. Sometimes the tongues of prisoners were cut off before they were executed by being flayed alive. At other times the eyes of prisoners were gouged out with lances while their heads were held in place with a cord passing through their tongues and/or lips and/or jaws.

After the victorious battles, Assyrian soldiers, accompanied by musicians, often played games of catch with the severed heads of their enemies. Such violence against the defeated foe was justified in the eyes of the Assyrians as it was seen as divine retribution for those that had rebelled against the King of Assyria and his gods.

We know how cruel the Assyrians were, not only from their own writings, but also from the carved stone reliefs that King Sennacherib made of his army's attack on, and his defeat of the city of Lachish in 701 BC and which he had erected in his palace in his capital, Nineveh. These reliefs, which are the nearest thing to a series of photographs of an Assyrian army attack on a city, now reside in the British Museum in London and are well worth a visit to see how the Assyrian army attacked and subdued its enemies. Lachish was built upon a hill with its main city walls built along the upper edge of the hill—these walls were 20-foot (6 metres) thick. The city was also surrounded by an outer retaining wall which was positioned mid-slope. Both walls were constructed of stone lower courses with the upper sections and battlements being built using mudbricks. The walls were separated by a smooth bank, known as a *glacis*, and were connected on the south-western side of the city by the largest double gates in the Southern Kingdom of Judah. Inside the city lay a massive palace-fortress complex that was the largest known structure in any city in the Southern Kingdom of Judah, including Jerusalem. Lachish presented a great challenge for King Sennacherib and his army, not only because of its double-wall fortification and natural defensive position set on a hill, but also because of the determination of its inhabitants to defend their city at all costs.

As with all Assyrian military attacks on major towns and cities, the siege of Lachish began with Assyrian envoys riding up to the city walls to demand its inhabitants to surrender. The Assyrians reminded the residents of Lachish that if they did so, they would be treated well but, if they resisted, they would suffer the common fate of all who had resisted the Assyrian army before them. Even though it was well-known that the Assyrians showed no mercy, the defenders of Lachish chose to take their chances and try to defend their city against the Assyrian attack. The envoys returned to the Assyrian encampment and the siege of Lachish commenced. Using the carved stone reliefs, which are now in the British Museum and which depict the siege of Lachish by the Assyrians, Dr Simon Anglim, a Military Historian at the Department of War Studies at King's College, London, has described the siege of Lachish as follows:

> The city was first surrounded to prevent escape. Next, archers were brought forward; under the cover of giant shields, they cleared the battlements. The king then used the tried-and-tested Assyrian method of building an earthen ramp close to the enemy wall, covering it with flat stone and wheeling forward a machine that combined a siege-tower with a battering ram. The Assyrians then staged a two-pronged assault. The tower was wheeled up the ramp and the ram was brought to bear against the mid-section of the enemy wall. Archers in the tower cleared the battlements while bowmen on the ground pushed up close to the wall to cover an infantry assault with scaling ladders. The fighting appears to have been intense, and the assault probably took several days, yet eventually the Assyrians entered the city.[19]

After looting it, the Assyrian army set fire to Lachish and it burned so intensely that it left a three-foot (90 centimetres) layer of charred debris. The cost to the inhabitants of Lachish was truly enormous as the discovery of a nearby mass grave, containing the remains of about 1500 men, women and children, illustrates. In addition, many of its inhabitants were taken captive and transported back to Nineveh to become slaves in the Assyrian empire. The prophet Micah leaves us in no doubt why this dreadful destruction of Lachish took place: it was the judgement of God. Lachish was a military fortress and its inhabitants had relied on their own military might rather than on the Lord to defend it—see Micah 1:13.

Flushed with success, King Sennacherib sent 'a great army' together with three envoys[20] to King Hezekiah in Jerusalem to try to obtain a surrender from him. These envoys met King Hezekiah's representatives and told them to remind King Hezekiah how the inhabitants of all the countries that the Assyrians invaded had been defeated and that their gods had been of no help to them. They questioned whether the Lord would deliver King Hezekiah and the inhabitants of Jerusalem out of the hand of the King of Assyria. The incident of the Assyrian army going to Jerusalem is not only recorded in the Bible (2 Kings 18) but is also recorded on the Taylor Prism, which now resides in the British Museum in London. This six-sided, clay prism was discovered in 1830 by Colonel R. Taylor, who at the time was the British representative in Baghdad, in the ruins of ancient Nineveh—in the area known today as Nebi Yunus. The cuneiform writing on this hexagonal prism not only confirms the Biblical account of King Hezekiah paying tribute to King Sennacherib, but it also states that King Sennacherib shut up King Hezekiah 'like a caged bird' in Jerusalem. Confronted by King Sennacherib's envoys and their demand that he surrender to the Assyrians, King Hezekiah sent his servants to Isaiah the prophet to find out from the Lord how to respond. Through the prophet Isaiah, God told King Hezekiah not to be afraid, for King Sennacherib would hear a rumour that would cause him to return to his own land and there he would 'fall by the sword'.

King Hezekiah instructed his representatives not to respond to the Assyrian envoys and so the envoys returned to King Sennacherib empty handed. When they arrived back in Lachish, they discovered that King Sennacherib had received a message to inform him that the King of Cush[21] had set out to fight him and he was now at Libnah.[22] However, King Sennacherib managed to get instructions to his messengers that had returned from Jerusalem and he ordered them to return to Jerusalem and try again to get King Hezekiah to surrender. The messengers took with them a letter from King Sennacherib which they gave to King Hezekiah. On receiving this letter, King Hezekiah went to the Temple and he spread the letter out and prayed to the Lord and begged the Lord to save him and his people from King Sennacherib and the Assyrian army. The Lord heard his prayer and spoke to him through the prophet Isaiah to inform him that King Sennacherib would not even come into Jerusalem and that his army would not build a siege ramp against its walls in order to attack it and the Assyrian army would not even shoot an arrow in Jerusalem or use a shield there (2 Kings 19:32). Furthermore, the Lord said that King Sennacherib would return to his own country the way he came (2 Kings 19:33).

Isaiah's prophecy was fulfilled to the letter. King Sennacherib and his army never came to Jerusalem; they did not build a siege ramp against its walls; and they did not shoot an arrow or use a shield there. The reason for this is that, as we have seen, King

Sennacherib and his army left Lachish to fight against the Cushites at Libnah and the Bible records that the Angel of the Lord killed 185,000 soldiers of the Assyrian army (2 Kings 19:35). The phrase, 'the Angel of the Lord', is a *Theophany*—a visible manifestation of God. It was therefore the Lord himself who slew the Assyrian army. This slaughter is vividly described by Lord Byron in his famous poem, 'The Destruction of Sennacherib' in the following words:

> For the Angel of Death spread his wings on the blast,
> And breathed in the face of the foe as he pass'd,
> And the eyes of the sleepers wax'd deadly and chill,
> And their hearts but once heaved, and for ever grew still!

And then, finally:

> And the tents were all silent, the banners alone,
> The lances unlifted, the trumpets unblown.
> And the widows of Ashur are loud in their wail,
> And the idols are broke in the temple of Baal;
> And the might of the Gentile, unsmote by the sword,
> Hath melted like snow in the glance of the Lord!

We do not know exactly where this took place because the Bible does not tell us. Perhaps, one day, archaeologists will find the remains of these soldiers somewhere, just as they have found the remains of the 1,500 men, women and children who perished in the siege of Lachish. Interestingly, the Greek historian, Herodotus, mentions that a great number of King Sennacherib's army died but gives the bizarre explanation that their bow strings, quivers and the handles of their shields were all gnawed by mice![23] After the Lord had killed so many of his army, it is no wonder that King Sennacherib returned 'with shame of face to his own land' as recorded in 2 Chronicles 32:21. When he did return home to Nineveh, he could not boast of sacking Jerusalem, the capital city of the Southern Kingdom of Judah, that he had invaded, so he had reliefs made showing how he had defeated Lachish, the second city of the kingdom. Twenty years after he went home, King Sennacherib fell by the sword, just as Isaiah had prophesied in 2 Kings 19:7, assassinated by two of his sons in January 681 BC.

Summary and conclusion

In this chapter we have looked at the twenty-nine-year reign of the good and faithful King Hezekiah, who was the king of the Southern Kingdom of Judah from 715 BC until 686 BC. He was the son of the faithless King Ahaz and the Bible informs us that his mother was Abi, the daughter of Zechariah. The first thing that King Hezekiah accomplished when he began to reign over the Southern Kingdom of Judah was to arrange for the Temple to be cleansed and a Passover to be celebrated for the children of Israel from both the Southern Kingdom of Judah and the recently defeated Northern Kingdom of Israel. Immediately after the celebration of the Passover, all the high places as well as the pagan pillars and altars and Asherah poles were destroyed, together with the bronze serpent that Moses had made. Temple worship was re-introduced. King Hezekiah then rebelled against the Assyrians and struck down the Philistines as far as Gaza. In early 701 BC, King Hezekiah took ill and, after pleading in prayer with the Lord, was healed and the Lord gave him an extra fifteen years to live. Envoys brought a present from Merodach-baladan, the King of Babylon in exile, for King Hezekiah when they visited him after his healing in early 701 BC. Shortly afterwards, the Southern Kingdom of Judah was invaded by the Assyrians in spring 701 BC and the Lord destroyed the Assyrian army, with the result that King Sennacherib and what was left of his army returned home to Nineveh. In 696 BC, five years after his illness and healing, King Hezekiah appointed his twelve-year-old son, Manasseh, as co-regent. The reason for this co-regency was that King Hezekiah wanted to give his son, Manasseh, all possible training in leadership and hoped that such training would help him to be a good king, like his father. We shall see in the next chapter whether this strategy worked or not. King Hezekiah died in 686 BC at the age of fifty-four.

No biography of King Hezekiah, however short, would be complete without a brief understanding of the history of Assyria immediately before the beginning of his reign and also during his reign. The family tree of the Assyrian kings on page 70 shows that, when Tiglath-Pileser III died in 727 BC, his son, Shalmaneser V, began to reign and it was he who invaded the Northern Kingdom of Israel and besieged and conquered its capital Samaria in 723 BC, the year before he died in 722 BC. His brother, Sargon II, then reigned after him and he was the Assyrian king who was reigning when King Hezekiah began his reign in 715 BC. Surprisingly, until the middle of the 19th century, the only reference to King Sargon II was in the Bible—in Isaiah 20:1. The reason for this is that he died in battle in 705 BC while quelling a rebellion in Tabal, a province in central Anatolia, and his body was not recovered from the battlefield. Because of this, the Assyrians thought that he was out of favour with the gods and, as a result, his successor, his son Sennacherib, moved the capital to Nineveh. The old capital, Dur-Sharrukin, eventually became deserted and was covered by sand and dust and the knowledge of its existence, together with that of King Sargon II, gradually faded, until it was re-discovered by archaeologists in 1843. King Sennacherib reigned for twenty-four years until 681 BC, when he was assassinated by two of his sons—then his youngest son, Esarhaddon, the son of one of his concubine, Zakutu, became king.

I stated at the beginning of this chapter that one of the main purposes of my writing about the kings that we find in the Old Testament is to show that they were not figments of the imaginations by the people who wrote about them, but they were real people. This is certainly true of King Hezekiah, as we have seen. His existence is known not only from the pages of the Bible, but also from the records of the Assyrian kings. We know that King Hezekiah reigned over the Southern Kingdom of Judah and that his kingdom was invaded by King Sennacherib of Assyria; and that, in spite of King Sennacherib extracting an enormous tribute of gold and silver— over 57 million pounds in today's money—from him, and, in spite of shutting him up 'like a caged bird' in Jerusalem, King Sennacherib did not attack and destroy Jerusalem. He did, however, attack and destroy the second most important city in King Hezekiah's kingdom—Lachish. This is not only recorded in the Bible, but also on the famous Lachish reliefs, which are now located in the British Museum and which once lined King Sennacherib's palace at Nineveh.

For almost 2,500 years, one of the most important Assyrian kings—Sargon II—simply disappeared from history. This man was one of the most important kings of Assyria—the founder of the

Sargonid Dynasty which occupied the throne of the Assyrian Empire for over a hundred years. Here was a king who ruled over almost the entire, then-known world—yet he became forgotten and he disappeared from the pages of history, except for a small mention of him in an old book, the Bible, that almost no-one accepted as trustworthy history. It is interesting to ponder if, in 2,500 years' time, the names of Putin, Trump or Xi Jinping will be remembered or whether they, too, will have disappeared from the pages of history until some future archaeologist finds statues of them—as the traveller in Shelley's poem 'Ozymandias' found the remains of the statue of Pharaoh Rameses II that once stood 57 feet (17 metres) tall but now lay half-sunk in the desert sands. In 2,509 years' time, will the great cities of Beijing, London, Moscow or Washington DC be lost and covered with sand and dust like the cities of Dur-Sharrukin and Nineveh did in the mid-19th century? And if you do not believe me about people today not knowing the names of the kings who reigned 2,500 years ago over most of the then-known world, ask your next-door neighbour if they know who Tiglath-Pileser III was, or Sargon II or Sennacherib. I guarantee they will probably not have a clue! These people's lives are important—especially King Hezekiah who teaches us about being good, faithful and trusting the Lord even when he was ill or when he was under attack from his enemy.

NOTES

1   Prof. Joshua Mark, 'Sargon II' in: https://www.ancient.eu/Sargon_II/
2   The human-headed, winged bulls that guarded the palace of Sargon II are now located in the British Museum in London.
3   ESV *Study Bible*, (Wheaton, Illinois: Crossway Bibles, 2008).
4   Prof. Joshua Mark, 'Sargon II' in: https://www.ancient.eu/Sargon_II/

5 Xenophon, *Anabasis*, 3.4.10–12

6 We are informed in 2 Chronicles 28:1 that Ahaz was twenty years old when he began to reign and this was in 732 BC. He was therefore born in 752 BC and would have only been twelve years old in 740 BC when his son, Hezekiah, was born.

7 Taken from: Victor Harold Matthews, Don C. Benjamin, *Old Testament Parallels: Laws & Stories from the Ancient Middle East* (Paulist Press, 2006) ISBN 9780809144358 quoted in: https://en.wikipedia.org/wiki/Annals_of_Sargon_II

8 A.J. Monty White, *Rogues in Royal Robes,* (Leominster: Day One Publications, 2020), pp. 62–64.

9 William Whiston (translator), *Josephus – Complete Works* (London: Pickering & Inglis, 1964), Book IX, Chapter XII, para 3, p. 210.

10 This was in 715 BC some eight years *after* King Hoshea's death. There was therefore *no* overlap in the reigns of Hezekiah and Hoshea. However, as pointed out by Professor Edwin Thiele on pages 174–175 of his book, *The Mysterious Numbers of the Hebrew Kings,* the final editor of Kings did not understand the dual dating for King Pekah and, as a result, 'he began the twenty years of Pekah in 740 BC, the fifty-second year of Azariah. But the twenty years actually began in 752 BC. This was the same year when Menahem began. Having thrust the commencement of Pekah twelve years ahead, from 752 BC to 740 BC, the editor also thrust the beginning of Hoshea twelve years ahead, from 732 BC to 720 BC. In such a case the nine years of Hoshea would terminate in 711 BC, not in 723 BC as they actually did. But with Hoshea being given the terminal date of 711 BC his years would overlap those of Hezekiah, who began in 715 BC.' There would also be an overlap with King Ahaz, King Hezekiah's father. This explains the anomalies in the synchronisms in 2 Kings chapters 17 and 18.

11 As pointed out by Andrew Thomson in note 2 of chapter 9 in his book, *Opening Up 2 Chronicles,* (Leominster: Day One Publications, 2011), in the United Kingdom we might say, '… from Land's End to John O'Groats' – that is from the far south to the far north.

12 The story of the bronze serpent that Moses made is found in Numbers 21:4–9. The bronze serpent was erected on a pole so that anyone who looked at it would be healed and would not die from the bites of the snakes that God had sent in order to punish the Israelites for speaking against Moses. By the time of King Hezekiah, the Israelites had begun to worship it and were making offerings to it. In 2 Kings 18:4 we are told that this bronze serpent was called *Nehushtan* and the footnote to this verse in the esv points out that this word sounds like the Hebrew for both bronze and serpent.

13 Clive Anderson, *Sennacherib* in the series *Face to Face,* edited by: Simon J Robinson (Leominster: Day One Publications, 2007), p. 19.

14 Edwin R Thiele, *The Mysterious Numbers of the Hebrew Kings, New Revised edition,* (Grand Rapids, MI: Kregel, 1983), p. 176.

15 Taken from 'Hezekiah's Tunnel Re-Examined' by the Biblical Archaeology Society Staff published on 28 November 2020 at https://www.biblicalarchaeology.org/daily/biblical-sites-places/jerusalem/hezekiahs-tunnel-reexamined/

16 Amihai Sneh, Eyal Shalev and Ram Weinberger, 'The Why, How, and When of the Siloam Tunnel Re-evaluated', *Bulletin of the American Schools of Oriental Research,* 359 (2010) pp. 57–65.

17 Article entitled 'The Siloam Inscription and Hezekiah's Tunnel' by Christopher Rollston at https://www.bibleodyssey.org/en/places/related-articles/siloam-inscription-and-hezekiahs-tunnel. This is Christopher Rollston's translation.

18 https://www.poetryfoundation.org/poems/43827/the-destruction-of-sennacherib

19 Simon Anglim, et al, *Fighting Techniques of the Ancient World 3000 BC–AD 500,* (London: Amber Books, 2013).

20 Three Assyrian officers are listed as 'the Tartan, the Rab-saris, and the Rabshakeh' (2 Kings 18:17). The Tartan was the General of the Assyrian army; the Rab-saris was a high official (possibly a senior eunuch) in the palace; and the Rabshakeh was an army commander and spokesperson for King Sennacherib as he could speak Aramaic—the language spoken by the people of the Southern Kingdom of Judah.

21 *'Cush'* is a Hebrew term, broadly referring to the countries of the Upper Nile, south of Egypt.

22 This was a city-state in the area occupied by the tribe of Judah. Its exact location was unknown until February 2015 when archaeologists from Ariel University claimed that they had discovered its ruins during a hillside dig at Tel Burna, which is near a town in South Central Israel. For details, see: https://www.haaretz.com/archaeology/.premium-biblical-city-of-libnah-identified-1.5303117

23 George Rawlinson (*Translator*), *The History of Herodotus,* Book II, chapter 141, (Everyman's Library number 405, London: J M Dent, 1910), Volume 1, pp. 186–187.

7 King Zedekiah—final king of the Southern Kingdom of Judah

I n this penultimate chapter, I want us to look at the lives of the last seven kings of the Southern Kingdom of Judah who reigned in the last one hundred years of the kingdom's existence—from 686 BC, when King Hezekiah died and his son Manasseh began his sole reign, to the year 586 BC, when King Zedekiah, the last king of the Southern Kingdom of Judah, escaped from Jerusalem immediately before it was destroyed by the Babylonian army. If we look carefully at the family tree on page 165, it shows how these seven kings are all related to one other. It also shows that the monarchy passed via the usual father-son relationship—from Manasseh to Amon to Josiah to Jehoahaz—but then it passed to his younger brother Jehoiakim and then to Jehoiakim's son, Jehoiachin. After reigning for only three months, King Jehoiachin was taken captive to Babylon, where he was eventually released some thirty-six years later, in 561 BC and where he lived out the rest of his life, dining regularly with the King. Upon King Jehoiachin being taken captive to Babylon, the throne passed to Jehoahaz's youngest brother Zedekiah, who was Jehoiachin's uncle. The family tree also gives the different names by which the kings were called and the dates when they reigned. It will be useful to keep referring to this family tree while reading this chapter about the lives of these kings, who were the last kings of the Southern Kingdom of Judah.

Seven kings reigned during the last hundred years of the Southern Kingdom of Judah. However, the length of the reigns of Manasseh (forty-four years) and Josiah (thirty-one years) account for seventy-five of these years. The other five monarchs only reigned for a total of twenty-five years—so each of their reigns was quite short, even though much happened during the times they occupied the Throne of David, as we shall see.

Hezekiah's wicked and repentant son, King Manasseh

I once heard or read somewhere that it is amazing what people believe so long as it is not in the Bible—and this is true about what some people believe about the mother of King Manasseh. In 2 Kings 21:1, we are informed that King Manasseh's mother's name was Hephzibah. A Google search of her informs us, via a number of websites, that she was the daughter of the prophet Isaiah. Apparently Isaiah rebuked King Hezekiah when he was ill for being unmarried and not having any children and so, as a result, King Hezekiah married Hephzibah.[1] But, in the Bible, there is *no record whatsoever* of Hephzibah being Isaiah's daughter and there is *no mention whatsoever* of King Hezekiah being reprimanded by Isaiah for being unmarried and childless when he was ill. Furthermore, had King Hezekiah married Hephzibah when he was ill (or immediately afterwards) that would have been in 701 BC and therefore his son, Manasseh, would have been only four years old (allowing for almost a year's gestation) in 696 BC when he became co-regent. However, the Bible informs us in 2 Kings 21:1 that

Manasseh was actually twelve years old when he became co-regent. The moral of this story is not to believe all you read on Google and keep checking and rechecking your facts.

To repeat, for the sake of clarity, the Bible informs us in 2 Kings 21:1 that Manasseh was twelve years when he was appointed as co-regent with his father, King Hezekiah. This was in the year 696 BC and he reigned over the Southern Kingdom of Judah for fifty-five years—ten years as co-regent with his father (from 696 BC to 686 BC) and forty-five years as sole ruler (from 686 BC to 642 BC).[2] This is longer than any other king reigned over the Southern Kingdom of Judah or even over the Northern Kingdom of Israel and it is longer than either King David or King Solomon reigned over the United Kingdom of Israel. The reason for his appointment as co-regent was that, presumably, King Hezekiah wanted to give Manasseh all possible training in leadership and he hoped that such training would help him to be a good king, like his father. However, this did not happen, for King Manasseh led his subjects astray 'to do more evil than the nations had done whom the Lord destroyed before the people of Israel' (2 Kings 21:9).

King Manasseh's reign can be divided into three parts. The first part, which lasted for ten years, was when he was co-regent with his father, King Hezekiah. Nothing is written in the Bible about him during this part of his reign—presumably he looked on and saw how well his father ruled. When his father died in 686 BC, King Manasseh rebelled against God and began to undo all the good that King Hezekiah had done and he began to do evil. In 2 Kings 21 and in 2 Chronicles 33, we are informed that King Manasseh:

- Rebuilt the high places that King Hezekiah had destroyed.

- Erected altars for Baal worship.
- Made a carved image of Asherah (the so-called *Queen of Heaven*), as Ahab, King of the Northern Kingdom of Israel had done, and set it up in the Temple.
- Worshipped and served the stars.
- Built pagan altars in Jerusalem.
- Built altars for star worship in the Temple.
- Burned his sons as offerings, presumably to Molech, in the Valley of the Son of Hinnom.
- Used fortune telling.
- Used omens.
- Used sorcery.
- Dealt with mediums.
- Dealt with necromancers.
- Shed much innocent blood.

According to the *Talmud*, a collection of Jewish texts that record the oral tradition of the early rabbis, some of the innocent blood that was shed was that of the prophet Isaiah. The prophet apparently hid inside a cedar tree and then was sawed in two by King Manasseh.[3] In the Heroes of the Faithful in Hebrews 11, we read about the people 'of whom the world was not worthy' (v. 38) and, in verse 37 of this chapter, we read of some, that 'they were sawn in two'. It is thought that this is a reference to the traditional account of the death of Isaiah, found in the early Jewish and Christian extra-biblical literature.[4]

But King Manasseh's evil actions and practices did not go unnoticed by the Lord and he sent prophets to warn the people that he would bring disaster upon Jerusalem and the Southern Kingdom of Judah because of the sins of King Manasseh and the fact that the people had also sinned by worshipping the idols that King Manasseh had made and erected. The Lord used the Assyrians to accomplish this disastrous blow on King Manasseh. We do not know the exact year of this invasion because the Bible does not give us any chronological references. The Assyrian records do not help us either as the Assyrian kings, Esarhaddon (681–669 BC) and Ashurbanipal (669–c631 BC), both claim that King Manasseh paid tribute to them.[5] The Bible tells us that the commanders of the Assyrian army captured King Manasseh and took him 'with hooks[6] and bound him with chains of bronze and brought him to Babylon' (2 Chronicles 33:11). It was in Babylon (some 550 miles [885 kilometres] as the crow flies from Jerusalem) that the third part of King Manasseh's reign began, for it was while he was a captive and 'in distress' (2 Chronicles 33:12) that he prayed to God. What follows is not only an amazing story of God's forgiveness, mercy and restoration but also a story of a completely changed heart in the life King Manasseh.

After all the evil and idol worship that King Manasseh had engaged in, the Lord heard his prayer and forgave him and King Manasseh was taken back to Jerusalem to reign again over the Southern Kingdom of Judah. But this time, he served the Lord God—he removed the foreign gods and idols from the Temple; he removed all the foreign altars that he had built in the area around the Temple and in all Jerusalem; and he restored the altar of the Lord in the Temple and offered on it peace and thanksgiving offerings to the Lord. King Manasseh also carried out building work in Jerusalem (see 2 Chronicles 33:14) and he put commanders of the army in all the fortified cities of the Southern Kingdom of Judah. After his return from his capture by the Assyrians and his imprisonment in Babylon, it can truly be said of this king that he knew God had forgiven him and he showed his thankfulness to the Lord by his actions—he even commanded the people in his kingdom 'to serve the Lord, the God of Israel' (2 Chronicles 33:16).

Manasseh's wicked son, King Amon

When King Hezekiah died, he was buried with the kings who had reigned over the Southern Kingdom of Judah but when his son, King Manasseh, died, he was buried in his own garden. It would appear that there was not much respect for the monarchy when King Manasseh's son, Amon, ascended the throne in 642 BC. The Biblical account of the reign of King Amon takes up just a few verses of Scripture—a mere eight verses in 2 Kings 21, and just five verses in 2 Chronicles 33. The accounts of his reign in both places are almost identical—the account in 2 Kings giving slightly more information, such as the name of his mother and where he was buried.

The story of King Amon's two-year reign over the Southern Kingdom of Judah, although short, makes very sad reading. He did not follow the Lord, but he served and worshipped the idols that his father had erected and served during the first part of his reign. King Manasseh's repentance had no effect on his son, King Amon, for, as the Bible puts it, 'this Amon incurred guilt more and more' (2 Chronicles 33:23). After a reign of only two years, King Amon was assassinated by his servants and these servants, in turn, were murdered by 'the people of the land' (2 Chronicles 33:25), who then made King Amon's eight-year-old son, Josiah, king in his place. King Amon was buried in the same garden as his father, King Manasseh.

Good King Josiah

In this section I want us to look at the reign of King Josiah, who was the son of the wicked King Amon and who reigned for thirty-one years from 640 BC to 609 BC. The Bible informs us that 'he did what was right in the eyes of the Lord, and walked in the ways of David his father; and he did not turn aside to the right hand or to the left' (2 Chronicles 34:2). In fact, he was still a boy when, in the eighth year of his reign—when he was only sixteen years old—he began to seek the God of his father David. Four years later, King Josiah began to cleanse Jerusalem and the Southern Kingdom of Judah of the carved idols, the altars of Baal and the Asherah poles that the people were using to worship their false gods instead of the Lord.

Six years later, at the age of twenty-six, Josiah began to organize the restoration of the Temple using money collected not only from the tribes of Judah and Benjamin in his own Southern Kingdom of Judah, but also from the tribes of Manasseh and Ephraim and from all the remnant of the Northern Kingdom of Israel (2 Chronicles 34:9). During this restoration, Hilkiah, the high priest, found what is described in 2 Chronicles 34:14 as 'the Book of the Law of the Lord given through Moses'. This was probably the whole or part of the Book of Deuteronomy, for in that book it refers to itself as 'this Book of the Law' no less than three times (Deuteronomy 29:21; 30:10; & 31:26). Hilkiah gave the book to Shaphan, the secretary, and he took it to King Josiah and began to read it to him. When the King heard

More Rogues in Royal Robes **163**

the words which were written in this Book of the Law, he tore his clothes for he realized that the Lord's wrath was kindled against the people of the Southern Kingdom of Judah because they had not obeyed the words which were written in this Book of the Law, being read to him. King Josiah then commanded his closest servants to enquire of the Lord for him—presumably to find out what the Lord wanted him to do. Through Huldah, the prophetess, the Lord told the King's servants to give the King two messages. The first message was that the Lord was going to bring disaster on the Southern Kingdom of Judah and on its inhabitants because they had forsaken the Lord and had made offerings to other gods. The second message was that they were to tell King Josiah that, because he had humbled himself and torn his clothes and repented and wept before the Lord, then the Lord would take him to his grave so that he would not see the disaster that the Lord was going to bring upon his kingdom.

Upon hearing the Word of the Lord given by Huldah, the prophetess, King Josiah continued his cleansing of his kingdom from idol worship. The high places, the Asherah images, the idols and the altars of Baal were removed and destroyed. He had the idols and altars ground to dust and then scattered over the graves of those who had sacrificed to these idols or had sacrificed on these altars. He also burned the bones of any priest that had sacrificed to these idols or had sacrificed on the altars. King Josiah then gathered all the inhabitants of his kingdom in Jerusalem and read to them the words of this *Book of the Law* and he then entered into a covenant with the Lord 'to walk after the Lord and to keep his commandments and his testimonies and his statutes, with all his heart and all his soul, to perform the words of the covenant that were written in this

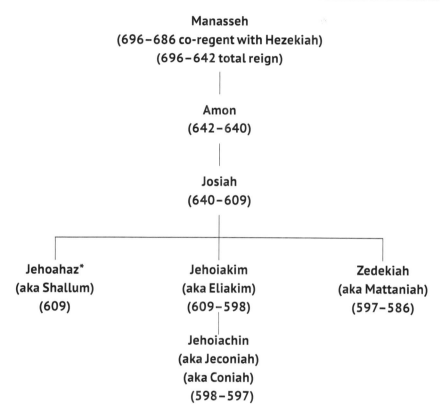

FAMILY TREE OF THE KINGS WHO REIGNED OVER THE SOUTHERN KINGDOM OF JUDAH FROM 696 BC TO THE FALL OF JERUSALEM IN 586 BC

Manasseh
(696–686 co-regent with Hezekiah)
(696–642 total reign)

Amon
(642–640)

Josiah
(640–609)

Jehoahaz*
(aka Shallum)
(609)

Jehoiakim
(aka Eliakim)
(609–598)

Zedekiah
(aka Mattaniah)
(597–586)

Jehoiachin
(aka Jeconiah)
(aka Coniah)
(598–597)

*Jehoahaz was not the eldest son, but the youngest. However, as he reigned immediately after his father, for the sake of clarity with respect to the order in which Josiah's sons reigned, he has been placed here.
All dates are BC.

book' (2 Chronicles 34:31). The Bible records, in both 2 Kings 23 and 2 Chronicles 34, that all the people of the land joined in the covenant, although, in 2 Chronicles 34:32, it states that King Josiah *made* the people join in the covenant, giving the impression that not all the people did so voluntarily.

Shortly afterwards, King Josiah celebrated a Passover. Unlike that held by King Hezekiah, this Passover followed the rules laid down in the Law and 'as prescribed in the writing of David King of Israel and the document of Solomon his son' (2 Chronicles 35:4). In 2 Chronicles 35:18 we are informed that this Passover was better than any Passover that had been celebrated in Israel since the days of Samuel the prophet—that would have been over four hundred years previously— and also that it was better than any that had been celebrated by any of the kings of Israel.

The historical books in the Old Testament are silent about the next thirteen years of the reign of King Josiah, apart from informing us that, after the Passover, King Josiah 'prepared the temple' (2 Chronicles 35:20). Then, in the summer of 609 BC, the Egyptian army, led by Pharaoh Necho II, travelled from Egypt to Harran, the recently established capital of the Assyrian Empire. This was on the road that led from Nineveh to Carchemish. Pharaoh Necho's plan was to join forces with the weakening Assyrian Empire against the increasingly powerful Neo-Babylonian Empire. The journey from Egypt to Harran led through the Southern Kingdom of Judah and it was this Egyptian army which King Josiah attempted to stop at Megiddo. Pharaoh Necho sent envoys to meet him and they explained to King Josiah that Pharaoh Necho was not at war with him but with the Babylonians, and that the Lord was with Pharaoh

Necho and King Josiah should cease opposing the Lord lest the Lord should destroy him. However, King Josiah did not listen to Pharaoh Necho who, according to the Bible, was speaking 'from the mouth of God' (2 Chronicles 35:22) but took his army to the plains of Megiddo where he was shot and wounded by an archer. King Josiah was taken back to Jerusalem by his servants in a chariot and there he died from his wounds at the age of thirty-nine and was buried in the tombs of his fathers. The story of King Josiah's conversation with Pharaoh Necho's envoys, his being wounded in battle and his subsequent journey back to Jerusalem where he died and was buried is recorded in 2 Chronicles 35:20–27.

Kings Jehoahaz, Jehoiakim and Jehoiachin

During the last quarter of the 7th century BC and the first half of the 6th century BC, so much chronological information is given in the Bible and in the Babylonian records that it allows us to follow the history of the reigns of these three kings of the Southern Kingdom of Judah and of the reigns of King Nabopolassar and his son, Nebuchadnezzar, of Babylon in detail. These three kings of the Southern Kingdom of Judah are closely related to each other, as the family tree on page 165 shows—Jehoahaz and Jehoiakim were brothers and Jehoiachin was the son of Jehoiakim and hence, he was also the nephew of Jehoahaz.

In chapter five we saw that the solar eclipse that took place on 15 June 763 BC is very important from a chronological standpoint, as it allows us to determine the dates of the reigns of the following kings: Shalmaneser III, Tiglath-Pileser III and Sennacherib of Assyria; Ahab, Jehu, Menehem, Pekah and Hoshea of the Northern Kingdom of Israel; and Uzziah, Ahaz and Hezekiah of the Southern Kingdom of Judah. Another, equally important eclipse took place on 22 April 621 BC. This was an eclipse of the moon and this took place in the fifth year of the reign of King Nabopolassar, who was the first king of the Neo-Babylonian Empire. Babylonian records show that he reigned from November 626 BC and died on 16 August 605 BC in the twenty-first year of his reign. The year of his death and the accession of his son, Nebuchadnezzar, who was his successor, is also confirmed by yet another astronomical event—another lunar eclipse which occurred in the thirty-seventh year of King Nebuchadnezzar's reign. As this eclipse occurred on 4 July 568 BC, this confirms that Nebuchadnezzar became king in 605 BC (on 7 September, to be precise). The dates of these two lunar eclipses also confirm the year (605 BC) that the prophet Daniel and his companions were taken from Jerusalem into captivity to Babylon.

To understand fully why the kings of the Southern Kingdom of Judah behaved the way they did, we have to appreciate the alliances and wars that were happening between the three major world powers at the time—Assyria, Babylon and Egypt. We have already seen that, in the summer of 609 BC, the Egyptian army, led by Pharaoh Necho II, travelled from Egypt to Harran, the recently established capital of the Assyrian Empire. Pharaoh Necho's plan was to join forces with the weakening Assyrian Empire against the increasingly powerful Neo-Babylonian Empire. The journey led through the Southern Kingdom of Judah and it was this Egyptian army which King Josiah attempted to stop at Megiddo and which resulted in his death. Jehoahaz (aka Shallum), the youngest son of King Josiah, was then made king by 'the people of the land' (according to 2 Kings 23:30 and

2 Chronicles 36:1) in his place.[7] The phrase, 'the people of the land', is probably a reference to what today we would call the elder statesmen of the kingdom. The Assyrian-Egyptian army was defeated by the Babylonian army at Harran and Pharaoh Necho II and his army made their way back to Egypt. When he reached Riblah, which is about 300 miles (about 500 kilometres) north of Jerusalem and is situated on the eastern bank of the Orontes River, he summoned the twenty-three-year-old King Jehoahaz to meet him and here Pharaoh Necho II captured him and took him prisoner to Egypt where he died in exile, thus fulfilling the prophecy of Jeremiah which is recorded in Jeremiah 22:11–12. Pharaoh Necho II made Jehoahaz's older brother, Eliakim, king instead and changed his name to Jehoiakim, and this is the name by which he is usually known. When Pharaoh Necho II deposed King Jehoahaz, he exacted a tribute from the Southern Kingdom of Judah of over one and a half million pounds in gold and over two million pounds in silver, in today's money. King Jehoiakim raised this tribute from his subjects, 'from everyone according to his assessment'—in other words, from taxation—according to 2 Kings 23:35.

This was the beginning of the end of the Southern Kingdom of Judah and of the reigns of the kings who sat on the Royal Throne of David in Jerusalem. Who reigned in Jerusalem was now in the hand of the empire who ruled the Southern Kingdom of Judah. At the beginning of King Jehoiakim's reign, the Babylonian army began to drive westward from Babylon towards the Mediterranean and southward towards Egypt. This southward drive resulted in the Babylonians, rather than the Egyptians, having control over the Southern Kingdom of Judah. As a result, Jerusalem was attacked by Nebuchadnezzar and the Babylonian army in 605 BC. This is recorded in Daniel 1:1–4, where we read that vessels from the Temple and members of the royal family (including Daniel and his companions), together with members of the nobility and the well-educated young people, were taken captive to Babylon. The prophet, Jeremiah, had repeatedly warned the people of the trouble and disaster that awaited them if they did not serve the Lord but continued to follow in their wicked ways.

King Jehoiakim reigned for eleven years from 609 BC to 598 BC and the Bible teaches that he did evil in the sight of the Lord. One of the most shockingly evil acts that he did is recorded in Jeremiah 36.[8] In the fourth year of King Jehoiakim's reign—in 605 BC—the Lord spoke to the prophet Jeremiah and told him to write down on a scroll all the words that the Lord had spoken to him, since the Lord had started to speak to him in the days of King Josiah. The prophet Jeremiah obeyed the Lord and dictated the prophecies to Baruch, who acted as his scribe. Jeremiah then ordered Baruch to read out these prophecies in the Temple—this did not occur, however, until the following year when the people gathered for a fast. Jeremiah asked Baruch to do this because at the time, Jeremiah was barred from entering the Temple and so was unable to read out the prophecies in person. The respected author and Bible teacher, Michael Wilcock, takes up the story:

'A big assembly had been called, perhaps because of the looming political crisis as the Babylonians took over the kingdoms of Palestine. In the crowd was a grandson of Shaphan's, Micaiah, who instantly grasped the importance of what he heard, and ran to the government offices where Jehoiakim's cabinet, of which his father was a member, was in session. In consternation they heard Micaiah's report, then sent for Baruch to bring the scroll and read the actual words. The nub of the matter was that Babylon was the 'foe from the north' with whom Jeremiah had so often threatened Yahweh's rebellious people, and that the kingdom's doom was at hand. This was dynamite. The cabinet advised Baruch that for their own safety he and Jeremiah should go into hiding, while they went to tell the king what was happening.'[9]

When King Jehoiakim heard what was being read to him, he took a pen knife and cut off that specific portion and threw it into the fire which was burning in the fire pot before him. This event took place in December 604 BC. No wonder the Bible states that he did evil in the sight of the Lord! Yet this king was not struck down dead by the Lord when he committed this wicked act—the Lord allowed him to live for another six years—until 598 BC.

During his reign, this evil king kept changing his allegiance from Egypt to Babylon and back again, depending on who he thought would better look after him and his ever-decreasing Southern Kingdom of Judah. At the beginning of this section, we saw that Jehoiakim was made king of the Southern Kingdom of Judah in 609 BC by the Egyptian Pharaoh Necho II. However, King Jehoiakim changed his allegiance from Egypt to Babylon in 605 BC (this was the year before he burned the scroll containing Jeremiah's prophecies) when Nebuchadnezzar besieged Jerusalem after the Babylonian army had defeated the Egyptian army at the Battle of Carchemish. King Jehoiakim changed his allegiance from Egypt to Babylon to prevent Jerusalem from being destroyed. However, it was at a cost: vessels from the Temple and members of the royal family (including Daniel and his companions), together with members of the nobility and the well-educated young people were taken captive to Babylon. Yet, four years later—in 601 BC—King Jehoiakim changed his allegiance back from Babylon to Egypt and this resulted in Nebuchadnezzar and his Babylonian army besieging Jerusalem some three years later in 598 BC. The Bible informs us, in 2 Chronicles 36:6, that Nebuchadnezzar bound King Jehoiakim 'in chains to take him to Babylon' but Nebuchadnezzar did not take him to Babylon. Jeremiah the prophet had prophesied (in Jeremiah 36:30) that King Jehoiakim's dead body would be 'cast out to the heat by day and the frost by night' and it would appear that this is what happened to him. Edwin Thiele has shown that King Jehoiakim died on 9 December 598 BC and this is the time of year when there is sun by day and frost by night in Jerusalem.[10] According to the Jewish historian Josephus, King Nebuchadnezzar had King Jehoiakim killed and had his body 'thrown before the walls, without any burial'.[11] So, although King Nebuchadnezzar had King Jehoiakim bound, ready to be taken captive to Babylon, he actually killed King Jehoiakim while he was still in Jerusalem.

King Jehoiakim was succeeded by his son, Jehoiachin, who also did evil in the sight of the Lord and who reigned for only three months and ten days (2 Chronicles 36:9) over the Southern Kingdom of Judah that now consisted of just the one square mile of its capital city, Jerusalem. Edwin Thiele has shown that the *three-months-and-ten-day period* of Jehoiachin's reign was from 9 December 598 BC to 22 April 597 BC.[12] He has also pointed out that a Babylonian tablet has been found that states Nebuchadnezzar besieged Jerusalem and captured it on Saturday 16 March 597 BC and that the King (that would be Jehoiachin) was then taken captive and a new king (that would be

Zedekiah) placed on the throne.[13] This accords with what is recorded in the Bible in 2 Kings 24:10, 17 and 2 Chronicles 36:9.

The account, in 2 Kings 24, gives additional information about the people that were taken captive together with the 'spoils of war' from the city of Jerusalem to Babylon:

> And Nebuchadnezzar king of Babylon came to the city while his servants were besieging it, and Jehoiachin the king of Judah gave himself up to the king of Babylon, himself and his mother and his servants and his officials and his palace officials. The king of Babylon took him prisoner in the eighth year of his reign and carried off all the treasures of the house of the LORD and the treasures of the king's house, and cut in pieces all the vessels of gold in the temple of the LORD, which Solomon king of Israel had made, as the LORD had foretold. He carried away all Jerusalem and all the officials and all the mighty men of valor, 10,000 captives, and all the craftsmen and the smiths. None remained, except the poorest people of the land. And he carried away Jehoiachin to Babylon. The king's mother, the king's wives, his officials, and the chief men of the land he took into captivity from Jerusalem to Babylon. And the king of Babylon brought captive to Babylon all the men of valor, 7,000, and the craftsmen and the metal workers, 1,000, all of them strong and fit for war. (2 Kings 24:11–16)

King Jehoiachin was taken in chains to Babylon where he was imprisoned. From the information given in 2 Kings 25:27, he was released in the year that Evil-merodach,[14] son of Nebuchadnezzar began to reign—on 2 April 561 BC. As Edwin Thiele points out, 'this was just before the first celebration of the New Year festivities on the part of the new king—a fitting time for the release of political

Chapter 7

prisoners.'[15] King Jehoiachin became king of the Southern Kingdom of Judah on 9 December 598 BC at the age of eighteen and he was taken prisoner to Babylon the following spring. He languished in prison in Babylon for the next thirty-six years until he was eventually released on 2 April 561 BC. He was now fifty-four years old and here, in Babylon, some 550 miles (885 kilometres) from the place of his birth, Jehoiachin lived out the rest of his life, dining regularly with the King.

King Zedekiah, last king of the Southern Kingdom of Judah

We have just read about the Babylonian King, Nebuchadnezzar, and his army besieging Jerusalem and taking Jehoiachin prisoner to Babylon in the spring of 597 BC. King Nebuchadnezzar then placed twenty-one-year-old Mattaniah on the throne and changed his name to Zedekiah, which is the name by which he is usually known. From the family tree on page 165, we can see that Zedekiah (aka Mattaniah) is the third son of King Josiah (see 1 Chronicles 3:15). He and Jehoahaz had the same mother (Hamutal) so they were full brothers. Because they had the same father, Zedekiah was Jehoiakim's half-brother and Jehoiachin's half-uncle. The story of King Zedekiah, the last king of the Southern Kingdom of Judah, makes sad reading. His epitaph is similar to so many that were written about his forebears: 'He did what was evil in the sight of the Lord his God' (2 Chronicles 36:12).

Sometimes, leaders of nations do not learn from history. King Zedekiah certainly did not learn from his half-brother, King Jehoiakim, who had changed his allegiance from Egypt to Babylon, then back to Egypt and, as a result, had lost his life when Jerusalem was attacked by the Babylonians in 598 BC. This last change of allegiance (from Babylon to Egypt) on the part of King Jehoiakim had actually resulted in Zedekiah being made king, when his nephew, King Jehoiachin (who was King Jehoiakim's son), was taken captive to Babylon. But, after reigning for nine years, and against the advice of the prophet, Jeremiah, given in Jeremiah 37:9, King Zedekiah rebelled against the Babylonians and, as a consequence, the Babylonian army led by King Nebuchadnezzar besieged Jerusalem again. This siege lasted for eighteen months—it began on 15h January 588 BC and culminated with the beginning of the final sacking of Jerusalem on 14 August 586 BC. Let the respected author and Bible teacher, Michael Wilcock, take up the story:

> The eighteen-month siege was interrupted by news of a move by Egypt. Necho II's successor, Psamtik II, was a cautious ruler, but he had just been succeeded by a new pharaoh, Hophra, who was eager to stir up trouble in Palestine. The Babylonians' grip on the city was relaxed as they prepared for a threatened invasion; people in the capital were free to come and go, and no doubt took the opportunity to lay in extra provisions just in case, or even to move away altogether.[16]

But the threat from Pharaoh Hophra faded and the Babylonian army returned to Jerusalem and continued to besiege the city. It is obvious that, towards the end of the siege, the famine in Jerusalem was very severe because not only does 2 Kings 25:3 state that there was no food for the people, but the prophet, Jeremiah, in Lamentations 4:10, refers to mothers boiling their own children for food! Furthermore, the prophet, Ezekiel, prophesied, in Ezekiel

5:10, that one of the judgements the Lord would bring on Jerusalem was that fathers would eat their sons and *vice versa*.

The Babylonian army eventually broke through the northern walls and entered the city on 18 July 586 BC. This was when King Zedekiah, his family and what was left of his army escaped from Jerusalem and made their way towards Arabah, which is the geographical area south of the Dead Sea. The Babylonian army, however, chased after them and caught up with them on the plains of Jericho. King Zedekiah's army deserted him and the Babylonian army captured him and his family and took them 250 miles (400 kilometres) north to Riblah—which is on the eastern bank of the Orontes River in Syria –where King Nebuchadnezzar had set up his headquarters during his campaign against the Southern Kingdom of Judah. Here, King Zedekiah was blinded after seeing his sons put to death and he was then bound in chains and taken another 600 miles (about 960 kilometres) to Babylon, where he remained a prisoner until he died.

Meanwhile, Jerusalem's final destruction began a month after the Babylonian army had broken through its northern walls and King Zedekiah, together with his family and what was left of his army, had escaped. On 14 August 586 BC, Nabuzaradan, who had been appointed by King Nebuchadnezzar to destroy Jerusalem and raze it to the ground, began his task. We can read about this in Jeremiah 52:1–23. The Temple was set on fire and the King's palace was destroyed as were all the homes of the inhabitants of Jerusalem. The city walls were also broken down. The bronze pillars of the Temple were broken in pieces and, together with all the bronze, gold and silver vessels that were used in the Temple, were taken to

Babylon. Jerusalem was razed to the ground and most of its population and those who were left in the Southern Kingdom of Judah were taken captive and transported to Babylon—see Jeremiah 52:28–30. Only the poorest of the land were permitted to remain, to be vinedressers and ploughmen—see Jeremiah 52:16. Not everyone fled from Jerusalem when King Zedekiah and his entourage escaped, for we read, in Jeremiah 52:24–27, that Nabuzaradan rounded up various people including the high priest and his assistant, some soldiers, seven members of the King's council, and sixty men who are described as 'men of the people of the land'. He took this group of men to King Nebuchadnezzar at his headquarters in Riblah, where the King executed them.

When the Babylonians withdrew from the Southern Kingdom of Judah, King Nebuchadnezzar appointed Gedaliah as governor of the land. Many saw Gedaliah as a collaborator, for in 2 Kings 25:24, he encouraged the people to accept the rule of their captors, the Babylonians, and to serve their king. After a couple of months, Gedaliah was assassinated by Ishmael (who was of the royal family according to 2 Kings 25:25), accompanied by ten of his colleagues. Shortly after that, the people (including King Zedekiah's daughters) that had been left by Nebuzaradan with Gedaliah, took Jeremiah and forced him to go with them to Egypt where, according to a tradition preserved in extra-biblical sources,[17] Jeremiah was killed in about 570 BC by being stoned to death by his fellow countrymen.

Summary and conclusion

In this chapter, we have looked in detail at the last one hundred years of the existence of the Southern Kingdom of Judah. We have looked at the lives of the seven kings who reigned during this period and saw that, apart from King Josiah, the obituary for each of them would read the same: they lived evil lives and caused their subjects, God's chosen people, to lead sinful lives and not to follow the Lord.

In the previous chapter, we considered the good and faithful life of King Hezekiah and we saw that he made his son, Manasseh, co-regent when he was only twelve years old, presumably hoping that such training in leadership would help him be a good king, like his father. However, this did not happen for, when Manasseh became king ten years later after his father died, he led his subjects astray 'to do more evil than the nations had done whom the Lord destroyed before the people of Israel' (2 Kings 21:9). God punished King Manasseh by having him captured by the Assyrians and taken to Babylon, where he truly repented of his wicked ways. When he was released from prison, he returned home and he faithfully served the Lord, even commanding the people in his kingdom to serve the Lord, the God of Israel. But King Manasseh's repentance and reformed life had no effect on his successor, his son Amon, whose evil reign lasted only two years before he was assassinated by his servants.

King Amon's eight-year-old son, Josiah, became king in his place. King Josiah was a good king from the start—the only thoroughly good king that the Southern Kingdom of Judah had during the last hundred years of its existence. We saw that, at the age of sixteen, he began to seek the God of his father David; at the age of twenty he began to cleanse Jerusalem and the Southern Kingdom of Judah of idolatry; and at the age of twenty-six he organized the restoration of the Temple at Jerusalem. During this restoration, the high priest found the *Book of the Law*—the whole or part of the Book of Deuteronomy—and when the King heard the words which were written in this Book of the Law, he tore his clothes in repentance for he realized that the Lord's wrath was kindled against his people. As a result of consulting Huldah, the prophetess, the Lord informed King Josiah that he, the Lord, was going to bring disaster on the Southern Kingdom of Judah and on its inhabitants because they had forsaken the Lord and had made offerings to other gods but, because he had humbled himself and torn his clothes and repented, the Lord would take him to his grave so that he would not see the disaster that the Lord was going to bring upon his kingdom. King Josiah then gathered all the inhabitants of his kingdom in Jerusalem and read to them the words of the Book of the Law and he entered into a covenant with the Lord to walk after the Lord and to keep his commandments, his testimonies and his statutes, and made the people of the land join in the covenant. Shortly afterwards, King Josiah celebrated a Passover which was better than any Passover that had been celebrated in Israel since the days of Samuel the prophet and also better than any that had been celebrated by any of the kings of Israel.

In the summer of 609 BC, the Egyptian army, led by Pharaoh Necho II, travelled from Egypt to Harran, the recently established capital of the Assyrian Empire. Pharaoh Necho's plan was to join forces with the weakening Assyrian Empire against the increasingly powerful Neo-Babylonian Empire. The journey from Egypt to Harran led through the Southern Kingdom of Judah and it was this Egyptian army which King Josiah attempted to stop at Megiddo. Pharaoh Necho sent his envoys to meet King Josiah and pleaded with him not to oppose him for, in so doing, he was opposing the Lord. However, King Josiah did not listen to Pharaoh Necho but took his army to the plains of Megiddo where he was shot and wounded by an archer. King Josiah was taken back to Jerusalem by his servants in a chariot and there he died at the age of thirty-nine from his wounds.

King Josiah had three sons and one grandson who inherited the Throne of David and they were not good kings—all doing evil in the sight of the Lord. However, we saw that, to understand fully why these kings behaved the way they did, we have to appreciate the alliances and the wars that were happening between the three major world powers at the time—Assyria, Babylon and Egypt. In the summer of 609 BC, Pharaoh Necho II travelled with his army from Egypt to Harran, which was the recently established capital of the Assyrian Empire. He did this so he could join forces with the weakening Assyrian Empire against the increasingly powerful Neo-Babylonian Empire. The journey northward from Egypt led through the Southern Kingdom of Judah and it was this Egyptian army which King Josiah attempted to stop at Megiddo and which resulted in his death. Jehoahaz (aka Shallum), the youngest son of King Josiah, was then made king by the elder statesmen of the kingdom. The Assyrian-Egyptian army, however, lost to the Babylonian army at Harran and, on the way home, Pharaoh Necho II summoned King Jehoahaz to Riblah, where he captured him and took him prisoner back to Egypt—he died there in exile. Pharaoh Necho II made Jehoahaz's older brother, Eliakim, king instead and changed his name to Jehoiakim. At the beginning of King Jehoiakim's reign, the Babylonian army began to drive westward from Babylon towards the Mediterranean and southward towards Egypt. This southward drive resulted in the Babylonians, rather than the Egyptians, having control over the Southern Kingdom of Judah and, as a result, Jerusalem was attacked by Nebuchadnezzar and the Babylonian army in 605 BC, when members of the royal family (including Daniel and his companions), together with members of the nobility and the well-educated young people, were taken captive to Babylon.

King Jehoiakim reigned for eleven years and the Bible teaches that he did evil in the sight of the Lord. One of the most shockingly evil acts that he committed was to cut up and burn the scroll on which the prophecies of Jeremiah had been written. Even so, this king was not struck down dead by the Lord when he committed this wicked act and the Lord allowed him to live for another six years—until 598 BC. During his reign, this evil king kept changing his allegiance from Egypt to Babylon and back again, depending on who he thought would better look after him and his ever-decreasing Southern Kingdom of Judah. In 609 BC, King Jehoiakim was made king by the Egyptian Pharaoh Necho II and so, at first, his allegiance was to Egypt. However, he changed his allegiance from Egypt to Babylon when Nebuchadnezzar besieged Jerusalem, after the Babylonian army had defeated the Egyptian army at the Battle of Carchemish; King Jehoiakim changed his allegiance hoping that this would prevent Jerusalem from being sacked. However, four years later, in 601 BC, King Jehoiakim changed his allegiance from Babylon back to Egypt and, as a result, Nebuchadnezzar and his Babylonian army besieged Jerusalem in 598 BC—and this resulted in King Jehoiakim losing his life. King Jehoiakim was succeeded by his son, Jehoiachin, who was only eighteen years old when he became king. He reigned for only three months and ten days over the Southern Kingdom of Judah, which now consisted of just the one square mile of its capital city Jerusalem. King Jehoiachin was deposed by the Babylonians and taken in chains to Babylon, where he languished in prison for the next thirty-six years until he was eventually released in 561 BC at the age of fifty-four. After his release, this former king of the Southern Kingdom of Judah lived the rest of his life in Babylon, hundreds of miles from Jerusalem—the place of his birth and the capital from where he had reigned as king.

When King Nebuchadnezzar deposed King Jehoiachin, he placed twenty-one-year-old Mattaniah, the third and youngest son of King Josiah, on the throne and changed his name to Zedekiah. After reigning for nine years, and against the advice of the prophet Jeremiah, King Zedekiah rebelled against the Babylonians and, as a consequence, the Babylonian army, led by King Nebuchadnezzar, besieged Jerusalem again. This siege lasted for eighteen months and towards the end of the siege, there was no food left in the city and the famine was so severe that its inhabitants resorted to cannibalism. The Babylonian army eventually broke through the northern walls and entered the city and this was when King Zedekiah and his family escaped from Jerusalem. They were captured by the Babylonian army on the plains of Jericho and taken to Riblah, where King Nebuchadnezzar had set up his headquarters during his campaign against the Southern Kingdom of Judah. Here, King Zedekiah was blinded after seeing his sons put to death and he was then bound in chains and taken to Babylon, where he remained a prisoner until he died.

Jerusalem's final destruction began a month after the Babylonian army had broken through its northern walls. This was undertaken by Nabuzaradan, who had been appointed by King Nebuchadnezzar to destroy Jerusalem. The Temple was set on fire and the King's palace was destroyed, as were all the homes of the inhabitants of Jerusalem. The city walls were also broken down. The bronze pillars of the Temple were broken in pieces and, together with all the bronze, gold and silver vessels that were used in the Temple, were taken back to Babylon. Jerusalem was razed to the ground and most of its population, along with those who were left in the Southern Kingdom of Judah, were taken captive and transported to Babylon. Only the poorest of the land were permitted to remain—to be vinedressers and ploughmen. When the Babylonian army withdrew from the Southern Kingdom of Judah, King Nebuchadnezzar appointed Gedaliah as governor of the land. Many saw him as a collaborator because he encouraged the people to accept the rule of their captors, the Babylonians, and to serve their king. After a couple of months, Gedaliah was assassinated and, shortly afterwards, the people that had been left by Nebuzaradan with Gedaliah took Jeremiah and forced him to go with them to Egypt where, according to tradition, he was killed by his countrymen some sixteen years later. They had to force Jeremiah to go to Egypt because, through him, the Lord had warned the people that they were not to go to Egypt, but stay where they were—once again, we saw how disobedient the children of Israel were to the Word of the Lord.

Chapter 7

NOTES

1 See for example https://sites.rootsweb.com/~dearbornboutwell/fam1112.html

2 The difference in elapsed time between the years given in the text and in the Bible is due to the variance of calendar years and not incorrect chronology. Edwin Thiele, in his book, The Mysterious Numbers of the Hebrew Kings, (Grand Rapids, MI: Kregel, 1983), has a very useful footnote about this on pages 87–88. It reads as follows: 'The complexities of coordinating the New Years of the ancient calendars with the modern Julian calendar make it a common practice to date ancient events with two Julian years that contain the ancient date in question, for example 908/7 BC. In this work [and in 'More Rogues in Royal Robes'] a single date is generally used to simplify the discussion, but occasionally this approach is problematic. The same difficulties that are encountered between Tishri years and Nisan years are encountered when attempting to date ancient events in modern Julian years. In some instances when single dates are used for ancient events, the time span of Julian years will differ by one year from the elapsed time given in the ancient record. When studied carefully, it will be seen that this is because of the difference in calendars; it is not due to an incorrect chronology.'

3 https://www.gotquestions.org/how-did-Isaiah-die.html

4 Note on Hebrews 11:37 in ESV Study Bible (Wheaton, Illinois: Crossway, 2008), p. 2382.

5 James B Pritchard (Editor), Ancient Near East Texts Relating to the Old Testament [2nd edition], (Princeton University Press, 1955), pp. 291, 294.

6 This is the painful practice of putting a rope or a metal hook through the tongue and/or the lips and/or the jaw.

7 1 Chronicles 3:15 lists King Josiah as having four sons: Johanan, Jehoiakim, Zedekiah and Shallum, in that order. We do not know the name of the mother of Johanan; the name of the mother of Jehoiakim was Zebidah; and the name of the mother of both Zedekiah and Shallum was Hamutal. We know from Jeremiah 22:11 that Shallum was in fact King Jehoahaz, who Pharaoh Necho II took captive to Egypt where he died. It could well be that Jehoahaz was Shallum's throne-name just as Albert, the son of the UK's George V, used the throne-name of George VI.

8 I realize that 'one of the most shockingly evil acts' that I am about to recount may not appear shocking or evil to some of my readers. However, the story has to be appreciated in its historical setting. At the time, the Word of the Lord was considered to be holy and very precious and something that should be treated with great respect and reverence—certainly not something that should be cut to pieces and burned in a fire, as King Jehoiakim did to the prophecies of Jeremiah. Today, we are bombarded by news items on our television screens of babies dying of malnutrition, children being killed by sniper fire and people

being killed by bombs. In comparison, the story of King Jehoiakim cutting up and burning the scroll of the prophecies of Jeremiah may not appear to be 'shockingly evil', but in its day it was indeed a shockingly evil act.

9 Michael Wilcock, *In the Days of the Kings,* (Fearn, Ross-shire: Christian Focus Publications, 2010), pp. 158–159.

10 Edwin Thiele, *The Mysterious Numbers of the Hebrew Kings*, p. 187.

11 William Whiston (translator), *Josephus — Complete Works,* Book X, Chapter VI, para 3, (London: Pickering & Inglis, 1964), p. 217.

12 Edwin Thiele, *The Mysterious Numbers of the Hebrew Kings,* p. 187.

13 Ibid, p. 186.

14 His Akkadian name was Amel-Marduk.

15 Edwin Thiele, *The Mysterious Numbers of the Hebrew Kings,* p. 190.

16 Michael Wilcock, *In the Days of the Kings,* (Fearn, Ross-shire: Christian Focus Publications, 2010), p. 160.

17 https://www.britannica.com/biography/Jeremiah-Hebrew-prophet

8 King Jesus Christ, King of Kings

We saw in the last chapter how, in 586 BC, the Southern Kingdom of Judah came to an end and, together with its downfall, came the apparent demise of the Throne of David. Jerusalem, with its magnificent Temple that King Solomon had constructed using the materials stockpiled by his father King David, now lay in ruins. King Zedekiah, the last king of the Southern Kingdom of Judah, had been blinded after seeing his sons murdered by King Nebuchadnezzar and was now languishing in a prison somewhere in Babylon. Also, in a prison in Babylon was King Zedekiah's nephew, King Jehoiachin, who was the penultimate king of the Southern Kingdom of Judah and who had already been held captive in Babylon for eleven years—he would continue to be held captive for another twenty-five years until his release in April 561 BC.

On 8 January 585 BC, word of the fall of Jerusalem reached those who had been taken captive to Babylon.[1] Those captives, like Daniel, would have found comfort in what the Lord had said through the prophet Jeremiah—that the Babylonian Exile would only last for seventy years and then the Lord would bring his people back to their land.[2] The Word of the Lord can be trusted, for this actually happened! The Babylonians began to take inhabitants of the Southern Kingdom of Judah captive and transport them to Babylon in 605 BC. Seventy years counting from this date takes us to 535 BC—

so this is the date we should expect the exiles to return to their homeland. In 539 BC, the Persian King, Cyrus, overthrew the Babylonian King, Nabonidus, and took control of a vast empire, including the territories of the former kingdoms of the Northern Kingdom of Israel and the Southern Kingdom of Judah. In 538 BC, King Cyrus issued a decree that the exiles from the Southern Kingdom of Judah were free to return to their ancestral homeland. The first six chapters of the book of Ezra cover the first wave of these exiles who returned with their leaders, Zerubbabel and the priest, Jeshua, in 538–535 BC—some seventy years after members of the royal family (including Daniel and his companions), together with members of the nobility and the well-educated young people, had been taken captive to Babylon by Nebuchadnezzar.

Jesus Christ—a uniquely different King

The New Testament book, *The Gospel According to Matthew,* begins by tracing the genealogy of the Lord Jesus Christ from Abraham. In so doing, it records his descent from King David, his son Solomon and then via the kings of the Southern Kingdom of Judah—kings whose lives we have studied in this book. The life of King Jesus Christ, the one to whom God gave the throne of his father David (Luke 1:32), is in such sharp contrast to the lives of the kings from whom he was descended. The Lord Jesus Christ was totally different from his ancestors who sat on the Royal Throne of David. Reading about him in the four accounts of his life, written in the New Testament by Matthew, Mark, Luke and John, show emphatically that he did not:

- commit adultery as King David did
- arrange for anyone to be killed as King David did

- have hundreds of wives and, as a result, worship other gods as King Solomon did
- worship other gods as King Joash, Amaziah, Ahaz, Manasseh and Amon did
- make alliances with the enemy as King Jehoshaphat did
- kill his relatives so he could sit on the Throne of David as King Jehoram and Queen Athaliah did.

Furthermore, here was one who, unlike King Rehoboam, realized that a kingdom divided against itself will not stand (Mark 3:24–25); one who, unlike King Rehoboam, offers us a light burden (Matthew 11:30). King Jesus Christ was placed on the Throne of David by God himself (Luke 1:32), not by foreign kings as Jehoiakim and Zedekiah were—by the Egyptian Pharaoh Necho and the Babylonian King Nebuchadnezzar, respectively. Unlike his forefather, King Jehoshaphat, here was One who stood firm and did not enter into pacts and covenants with the enemy and who, unlike King Solomon and King Joash, faithfully worshipped and served his Father, the one true God, all the days of his life on this earth. Furthermore, the Lord Jesus Christ was never ill, like King Asa, King Uzziah and King Hezekiah.

At the end of Jesus' life, Pontius Pilate, the Roman Prefect (to give him his correct title) or Governor of the Roman Province of Judaea, said of Jesus, 'I find no guilt in this man,' and therefore found him not guilty of any of the charges that were made against him by the Chief Priest, the Elders, or the Scribes (see Luke 22:66; 23: 4,14). Compare this to what is written about King Amon, for example: he who 'incurred guilt more and more' (2 Chronicles 33:23). Finally, in this summary of the character of Jesus, we must let God have the last word. At Jesus' baptism, God said, 'This is my beloved Son, with whom I am well pleased' (Matthew 3:17). No wonder God, himself, spoke from heaven on the Mount of Transfiguration and told the disciples that were with Jesus that they were to listen to him (Mark 9:7). Through the pages of Scripture, God speaks to us today and tells us the same message—that we are to listen to what Jesus says. And we can listen to him telling us what to do with our lives by reading the Bible—his Word.

Nature or nurture?

According to Wikipedia the alliterative question, *Nature or Nurture?* has been in use in the English language since the Elizabethan period and has its origins in Medieval French.[3] It is asking the question: 'Is behaviour determined by the environment in which a person is brought up, or is it determined by a person's genes?' If I may be personal for a moment, when I was converted in the mid-1960s, I met a number of Christians who accepted what I consider to be the erroneous belief that curses and/or blessings are passed down through family lines. These people based this view on the fact that, as the Lord Jesus Christ was descended from King David, God had therefore chosen and blessed Jesus' line of descent. Conversely, they believed that God cursed other family lines, such as Saul's, so that, for example, none of his sons could become a king of Israel. You can see that this view is totally mistaken because you can point out that King David was an adulterer and a murderer and that other kings of his line, such as Ahaz and Amon, were totally evil and did not serve the Lord. However, Christians who held such a belief would ask me about my family ancestry and would be convinced that I must be from a long line of Christians. When I told them that my parents were atheists,[4] and that they did all they could to instil atheistic beliefs into me,[5] they were shocked and would then ask about my grandparents. When I told them that they, too, were either atheists or had no time for the Lord, they were even more shocked.

The fact that the Lord saved me is remarkable, for I was brought up in a household that really did have no time for God. My father was a very bitter atheist and yet, the Lord saved him when he was seventy-eight years old. His father (my paternal grandfather) married my grandmother (an alcoholic) when he was only sixteen years old using his uncle's birth certificate.[6] My grandmother died when my grandfather was in his sixties and he, then, married a woman who, by her own admission, was a white witch belonging to a coven, and he was married to her for almost twenty years. This grandfather—my paternal grandfather—was illegitimate. His father (my great grandfather) was training to be a Methodist Minister when he got my great grandmother pregnant and his family stopped him getting married to her by sending him to New York. Although he returned to the UK a few years later, not once did he try to contact my great grandmother or their son (my paternal grandfather).[7] In fact, he changed denominations—from Methodism to Anglicanism—and he then trained for the Anglican ministry in Durham. He finally ended up as an Anglican vicar in Leicester. Telling those who believe that blessings run in family lines about my White family, usually brings looks of shock and horror to their faces—more so if I go back a few generations and recount to them about the murderer and the brothel keeper in my ancestry! At least it gives me an opportunity to speak about God's grace in my life and how the Lord has saved so many of my family[8] since my conversion and used so many of my family in Christian ministry[9] since I was converted in 1964.

Those of us who are Christians, are not Christians because of nature—it has nothing at all to do with from which family we are descended. Furthermore, it has nothing at all to do with nurture, as the following paragraph will demonstrate. I am sure you can think of dozens of godly parents who have brought up their children in a good Christian home and have done all they can to ensure that their children will believe in God and accept the Lord Jesus Christ as their Saviour. Yet this is no guarantee that their children will follow God. Many of us see these children reject God and never pray to him, read his Word (the Bible) or worship him. So, if it is not nature or nurture that causes people to become Christians, what is it? The simple answer is 'God'.

Again, allow me to share my personal experience. When I was five years old, I heard the story recounted in 1 Samuel 3, about Eli the priest telling the young boy Samuel that he should say to God 'Speak Lord, for thy servant heareth' (v. 9, AKJV). I decided that I would pray this prayer to God and this became my constant prayerful desire— that the Lord would speak to me—in spite of my parents constantly telling me that there was no God and therefore he could not speak. I continued to pray this, even after the vicar of the local Anglican Church that I attended told me that God did not have anything to do with scruffy kids like me from the local council estate. Because of my parents constantly telling me that there was no God and also the rejection by the vicar of the local Anglican Church, in my mid-teens I drifted into atheism. But God had heard my prayer that I must have prayed thousands of times because, at the age of nineteen, God did speak to me. He told me I was a sinner and that I needed to be saved. God had already put someone by my side who was able to explain the way of salvation to me and, on 25 February 1964, I trusted the Lord Jesus Christ as my Saviour. This paragraph alone shows that salvation is of God. Why, as a five-year-old child, did I start praying asking God to speak to me? *That was of God.* As an atheistic teenager, why did I study the Old Testament in order to argue about its historicity with Christians? *That was of God.* Why did I end up going to university in Aberystwyth (the only university that offered me a place to study, by the way) and meeting someone who had the answers to all the questions I had about Old Testament history? *That was of God.* Becoming a Christian has nothing whatsoever to do with nature or nurture—*it is all of God.*

Clothed in his royal robes

The Lord Jesus Christ was born in Bethlehem and, according to early Christian tradition, he was born in a cave used for sheltering animals.[10] Mary, his mother, wrapped him in swaddling clothes and he was laid in a manger or animal feeding trough. King Jesus was not born in a palace and his first baby clothes were not fine royal robes fit for a king, but simple strips of cloth. The announcement of his birth was not heralded by royal courtiers blowing trumpets, the ringing of bells and a proclamation on a notice board in the Palace forecourt. God did one better—his birth was announced by an angel. But this pronouncement was not made in King Herod's palace in Jerusalem or in the place where the Jewish leaders met—it was made to a few shepherds who were looking after their sheep on a mountainside in Bethlehem. This was most likely on a mountainside where, over a thousand years before, Jesus' ancestor, David, had looked after his father's sheep before he was anointed King of Israel. These shepherds were probably looking after the sheep that would be used as the sacrificial lambs due to be sacrificed as atonement for sin by the people. God was obviously revealing that this baby, born in Bethlehem, was to be the Lamb of God who takes away the sins of the world.

My favourite nativity story is found in Luke chapter 2, about the time when Mary and Joseph took Jesus to the Temple to present Him, their first-born, to the Lord and to offer a sacrifice of a pair of turtledoves or two young pigeons. In the Temple, there was an old man, Simeon, and God had told him that he would not die until he saw God's provision of salvation. When I first read this story, after I had become a Christian, I was amazed, and I am still amazed, how this old man could take Jesus in his arms and say to God that he could now die in peace for he had now seen God's salvation. Think about it—he saw a baby and knew that this was God's means of salvation for the world! This is truly amazing! He did not hear Jesus preach or teach; he did not see Him perform miracles; he did not see Him die on the cross and rise from the dead. But Simeon knew that this little baby was the Saviour!

In spite of the title of my book, let me state clearly: King Jesus was not a rogue. Although, when he lived on the earth, he was tempted just like we are all tempted, he was 'without sin', as the writer of the book of Hebrews states emphatically (4:15). This may be difficult for us to imagine or even comprehend, especially when we remember that God's standards are so much higher than ours. For example, Jesus taught that if we lust after someone in our minds, this is equivalent to committing adultery with that person (Matthew 5:27–28) and therefore breaking the seventh Commandment. There are also sins of omission—'We have left undone those things which we ought to have done.'—to quote from the so-called General Confession which is found in the old *Book of Common Prayer* (1832). It seems that there is no hope for us because we have all sinned and we have all fallen short of God's standards. But this can never be said of Jesus—for he *never* sinned. He was guiltless, unlike the wicked son of the evil King Manasseh, King Amon, who incurred guilt more and more (2 Chronicles 33:23). Even Pontius Pilate attested that he found 'no guilt' in the Lord Jesus Christ— not once, but three times (John 18:38; 19:4 and 19:6). Yet, this sinless, guiltless man—the Lord Jesus Christ, the Son of God—was made to be a sacrificial offering on Calvary's cross so that those who trust in him may stand guiltless before God on the Day of Judgement (1 Corinthians 1:8). King Jesus offers us salvation—the taking away of our sins—and offers to replace our filthy rags of unrighteousness with his *Royal Robe* of righteousness.

There are literally thousands of millions who are clothed in these *Royal Robes* of righteousness. In my own family there is my wife, her mother, her brother, our children, my mum, my dad, my maternal grandmother, my sister, her husband and their children. And some of these are already in heaven in that great crowd of believers that no one can number. Jesus did not die for a few, but he died for the hundreds of millions who have trusted him as their Saviour and who can say that they may have been rogues, but now they are clothed in *Royal Robes*.

Summary and conclusion

After reading this book, I trust that you will have been persuaded that the kings you read about in the Old Testament, especially in the Books of Kings and Chronicles, were real people reigning over actual kingdoms and that they lived and died at the times recorded in these books. They were not mythological monarchs ruling over imaginary kingdoms but were real royals who lived in actual palaces which were located in cities that actually existed. They were kings of flesh and blood—cut them and they bled like we do—as some of them found to their cost when they were wounded, some fatally, in battles with their enemies. Even though they lived over 2500 years ago, we have seen them display the whole gamut of human emotions as we do, living in the 21st century: ambition, anger, covetousness, disappointment, forgiveness, greed, grief, happiness, hatred, hunger, impatience, jealousy, joy, loneliness, love, lust, pleasure, sorrow, temptation, thirst, tiredness, and weariness. And just as we do, they experienced aches and pains, illness and even death itself. In fact, they are all dead—with one notable exception, the Lord Jesus Christ, who rose from the dead after his crucifixion at Calvary.

We saw in the last chapter that the final destruction of Jerusalem began on 14 August 586 BC, a month after the Babylonian army had broken through its northern walls. The Temple was set on fire and was totally destroyed. Although this act of destruction was undertaken by the Babylonians, the enemy of God's people, it was an act in which the Lord was showing his people that a time was coming when there would be no need of a Temple to offer sacrifices for sin. This time came when the Lord Jesus Christ was crucified on the cross at Calvary—and offered himself, 'for all time a single sacrifice for sins' (Hebrews 10:12). This sacrifice was accepted by God and, after the Lord Jesus Christ rose from the dead, he ascended into heaven. There, in heaven, the Lord Jesus Christ sits on the Throne of David and is surrounded by a great multitude that no one can number from every nation, from all tribes and peoples and languages and they praise and worship with the words:

> Salvation belongs to our God who sits on the throne, and to the Lamb! (Revelation 7:10).

NOTES

1 Edwin Thiele, *The Mysterious Numbers of the Hebrew Kings* [New Revised edition], (Grand Rapids, MI: Kregel, 1983), p. 191.

2 Jeremiah 29:10–14.

3 https://en.wikipedia.org/wiki/Nature_versus_nurture

4 My mother became a Christian in September 1964, seven months after my own conversion and my father eventually became a Christian in October 1997 at the age of 78. I tell people that if they have a bitter, bad-tempered, cantankerous, self-righteous, God-denying relative like my father was, then they should keep praying for that relative because, if God can save my father, He can save anyone!

5 I often joke that my parents brought me up to be an atheist, but they failed miserably!

6 My grandfather altered or doctored this birth certificate as he was only 16 years old at the time of his marriage and his uncle was 26 years older but had been killed in the First World War. I think using an altered birth certificate, that was not his own, would make my grandfather's marriage illegal, to say the least.

7 If my great grandfather had contacted my great grandmother and if they had got married, then my family name would not be White, but it would be Watkin. However, if this had happened, then I would not exist, for, in 1940, my father would have been put on another ship from the one he was put on, and he would have been killed, as that other ship was sunk with no survivors—my father saw it happen. Fifty-one men trained together. When it was decided to what ship they were to be allocated, it was done in alphabetical order. The first forty-eight were put on the ship that was sunk. The next three (and my father was the

first of those three) were allocated to another ship and, as a result, my father survived the Second World War—although he had nightmares for the rest of his life about seeing that other ship explode and sink, killing forty-eight of his comrades with whom he had trained. Also, by not being on that other ship, my father met my uncle (my mother's brother) and, as a result of my uncle giving my father the address of my mother, he wrote to her, they met, got married and here I am! To me, this whole episode is a demonstration of what is written in Romans 8:28–30.

8 My father, my mother, my maternal grandmother, my sister and her husband and two daughters, my wife (when she was my girlfriend) and our three children.

9 A summary of my own involvement in Christian ministry can be found in 'About the Author' at the beginning of this book. My youngest son has been a Youth Leader and part of the team who manage the 'sound system' in the churches where he has been a member. My sister is a pastor's wife and is the Project Manager of their church. She and her husband have been involved in evangelistic work both at home and abroad. My sister's eldest daughter is a pastor's wife. My sister's youngest daughter is also a pastor's wife and she is responsible for the Worship and the Children's and Youth Work in their church.

10 Timothy Cross in an article entitled 'No Room at the Inn' published in *Evangelical Times* (December 2013) and available at: https://www.evangelical-times.org/21560/no-room-at-the-inn/

Appendix one

DATES OF THE REIGNS OF THE KINGS OF ISRAEL AND THE KINGS OF THE SOUTHERN KINGDOM OF JUDAH TOGETHER WITH THE DATES OF SIGNIFICANT EVENTS MENTIONED IN THIS BOOK		
All dates are BC. SKJ is the Southern Kingdom of Judah. NKI is the Northern Kingdom of Israel.		
King or Event	**Dates of Co-regency**	**Dates of Reign of King or Event**
Saul		1050–1010
David		1010–970
Solomon		970–930
Rehoboam		930–913
Split of Israel into the SKJ and NKI		930
Invasion of SKJ by Shishak		Spring 925
Abijah (aka Abijam)		913–910
Asa		910–869
Jehoshaphat	872–869	872–848 (total reign)
Jehoram	853–848	848–841 (sole reign)
Ahaziah		841
Athaliah		841–835
Joash		835–796
Amaziah		796–767
Azariah (Uzziah)	792–767 (overlap with Amaziah)	792–740 (total reign)
Bur Sagale Solar Eclipse		15 June 763

Jotham	750–740	750–732
Ahaz	735–732 (overlap with Jotham)	732–715 (official reign)
Fall of city of Samaria to Assyrians		723
Hezekiah		715–686
Sacking of Lachish by Assyrians		701
Manasseh	696–686	696–642 (total reign)
Amon		642–640
Josiah		640–609
Jeoahaz		609
Jehoiakim		609–598
Jehoiachin		598–597
Zedekiah		597–586
Babylonian army began to destroy Jerusalem		14 August 586
Jehoiachin released from captivity in Babylon		2 April 561

Appendix two

DATES OF THE REIGNS OF THE KINGS OF ISRAEL AND THE KINGS OF THE NORTHERN KINGDOM OF ISRAEL TOGETHER WITH THE DATES OF SIGNIFICANT EVENTS MENTIONED IN THIS BOOK

All dates are BC.

SKJ is the Southern Kingdom of Judah.

NKI is the Northern Kingdom of Israel.

King or Event	Dates of Co-regency	Dates of Reign of King or Event
Saul		1050–1010
David		1010–970
Solomon		970–930
Split of Israel into the SKJ and NKI		930
Jeroboam I		930–909
Nadab		909–908
Baasha		908–886
Elah		886–885
Zimri		885 (7 days)
Tibni		885–880
Omri	885–880 (kingdom divided with Tibni)	885–874 (total rule)
Samaria built and made capital of NKI		circa 880
Ahab		874–853
Shalmaneser III, King of Assyria		874–853

Battle of Qarqar – coalition including Ahab defeated by Shalmaneser III		853
Ethbaal (aka Ithobaal I) King of Phoenicia & father of Jezebel		born 915, died 847
Ahaziah		853–852
Joram		852–841
Jehu		841–814
Jehu paid tribute to Shalmaneser III of Assyria		841
Jehoahaz		814–798
Jehoash		798–782
Jeroboam II	793–782 (co-regent with Jehoash)	793–753 (total reign)
Bur Sagale Solar Eclipse		15 June 763
Zechariah		753 (6 months)
Shallum		752 (1 month)
Tiglath-Pileser III, King of Assyria		745–727
Menahem		752–742
Pekahiah		742–740
Pekah		752–732 (total reign)
Hoshea		732–723
Fall of city of Samaria to Assyrians		723

Note: Pekah was a rival to Menahem for 10 years and to Pekahiah for 2 years. He assassinated Pekahiah and his sole reign lasted for 8 years from 740 to 732.

Appendix three

Biblical chronologies often used by American theologians

As I stated in the Preface, in this book and in my previous book,[1] the dates given for the reigns of the kings of Israel, the Northern Kingdom of Israel and the Southern Kingdom of Judah are those that have been determined by Professor Edwin Thiele[2] who, incredibly, is relatively unknown. I pointed out in my previous book, and repeated in the Preface to this book, that this is surprising for this man achieved what no one else before him had— he established a detailed chronology from the data given in the Bible about the kings of the Northern Kingdom of Israel and the Southern Kingdom of Judah. It cannot be over-emphasized that this was no mean feat for, until Professor Thiele's achievement, no one could make the numbers given for the lengths of the reigns of the kings of the Northern Kingdom of Israel agree with those given for the reigns of the kings of the Southern Kingdom of Judah and *vice versa*. The chronology of the Hebrew kings formed part of Professor Thiele's doctoral programme at the University of Chicago and, until the publication of this research, the dates that were established from the Bible seemed to be at variance with those established from historical sources of the countries surrounding the land of Israel at the time.

Basically, Professor Thiele accomplished two outstanding feats. Firstly, he established a single chronology for both the Northern Kingdom of Israel and the Southern Kingdom of Judah that got rid of all the apparent discrepancies that existed between the chronologies of these two kingdoms. And secondly, he locked this chronology into the established chronologies fixed by modern astronomical records of the surrounding countries, notably those of Assyria and Babylon. Professor Thiele's work finally put all the pieces of the chronological jigsaw together for the period covering the reigns of the kings of the Northern Kingdom of Israel and the Southern Kingdom of Judah.

As already mentioned, in my books I use the dates established by Professor Edwin Thiele for the reigns of the kings of the Northern Kingdom of Israel and the Southern Kingdom of Judah. I also use the dates that he gives for the important events in the life of the nation of Israel. For example:

- that in 853 BC, King Shalmaneser III of Assyria fought a coalition of a dozen kings, including King Ahab of the Northern Kingdom of Israel, at the battle of Qarqar—an ancient town on the banks of the Orontes River, in north-western Syria,
- that 12 years later in 841 BC, King Shalmaneser III of Assyria received tribute from King Jehu of the Northern Kingdom of Israel, as depicted on the so-called *Black Obelisk*—which is now in the British Museum in London,
- that Samaria, the capital city of the Northern Kingdom of Israel, was sacked by the Assyrian army in 723 BC,
- that King Sennacherib of Assyria invaded the Southern Kingdom of Judah at the time of King Hezekiah in 701 BC,
- that the Babylonian army began to destroy the city of Jerusalem on 14 August 586 BC.

But these dates are not just the dates used by Professor Edwin

Thiele. They are the established dates accepted and used by Biblical scholars and theologians all over the world—with one exception, and that is by many in the United States of America.

There is a pool of Christian books published in the United States (and therefore read by Christians in the UK) that publish very confusing chronologies.[3] These books use the generally accepted dates for the reigns of the Assyrian kings, but then use totally different dates for Biblical events and the reigns of the kings of Israel, the Northern Kingdom of Israel and the Southern Kingdom of Judah than the ones that are accepted and used by Biblical scholars and theologians all over the world. It appears that these so-called Biblical dates are based on Ussher's chronology.[4] This chronology is interesting from a historical point of view, but so many Biblical and archaeological discoveries have been made since Archbishop Ussher lived, that the dates that he deduced for the Old Testament kings *have to be revised* in the light of these Biblical and archaeological findings.

The effect of using two chronologies—Ussher's chronology for the Biblical events and the so-called *established one* for the historical Assyrian events—leads to some bizarre conclusions. The first one I would like us to consider is that Tiglath-Pileser III and Pul were *not* one and the same individual. The English translation of the Authorised King James Version of 1 Chronicles 5:26 suggests that there were *two* Assyrian kings, Pul and Tiglath-Pileser (called Tilgath-pilneser in the AKJV), who invaded the Northern Kingdom of Israel and took the Israelites captive to different parts of the Assyrian Empire. However, the original Hebrew of 1 Chronicles 5:26 emphatically shows that Tiglath-Pileser and Pul were *one and the same person* because it reads: 'the God of Israel stirred up the spirit of Pul king of Assyria, and the spirit of Tiglath-Pileser king of Assyria, and he [singular] carried them [*that is some of the people of the Northern Kingdom of Israel*] away ....' The Hebrew verb, 'carried', is here in the singular and it is correctly translated with the singular pronoun, 'he'. This conveys the idea that Pul and Tiglath-Pileser III were names used for the same person and the correct translation of the '*waw*', introducing the phrase regarding Tiglath-Pileser, should be translated by the word 'even', as it is in all modern translations of the Scriptures.

The fact that Pul is another name for Tiglath-Pileser III is also borne out by the fact that Babylonian records have been discovered which show that his Babylonian name was Pulu and his Assyrian name was Tiglath-Pileser. Furthermore, this verse of Scripture is translated such that the two names are shown to belong to the same individual in *all* modern translations. In his book, *The Chronology of the Old Testament*, Dr Jones maintains that Pul is not Tiglath-Pileser III but is a totally different Assyrian king— Ashur-dan III.[5] The reason for this is because 2 Kings 15:19–20 records King Menahem of the Northern Kingdom of Israel paying tribute to King Tiglath-Pileser III. Because the Biblical chronology used by Dr Jones is incorrect, he maintains that King Menahem reigned 772–761 BC. The Assyrian records show that King Tiglath-Pileser III reigned 745–727 BC. So, according to the Biblical chronology in Dr Jones' book, there was no overlap in their reigns and so Pul could not be Tiglath-Pileser III in 2 Kings 15:19–20. *But* the dates given for King Menahem's reign by Dr Jones are incorrect. King Menahem actually reigned 752–742 BC and so, there was a three-year overlap (745–742 BC) with the reign of King Tiglath-Pileser III. King Menahem would have been able to pay tribute to King Tiglath-Pileser III during his reign.

Because the Biblical chronology used by Dr Jones in his book, *The Chronology of the Old Testament* is incorrect, Dr Jones does *not* accept that it is King Jehu who is depicted as paying tribute to the Assyrian King, Shalmaneser III, on the famous Black Obelisk, which is now in the British Museum in London. His rejection is based on three different reasons:[6]

- The *first* is that the date of those paying tribute to King Shalmaneser III is 841 BC and, according to Dr Jones' chronology, King Jehu reigned 885–857 BC—some sixteen to forty-four years *before* he could possibly have paid tribute. But Dr Jones' biblical chronology is incorrect. King Jehu actually reigned 841–814 BC and so, was reigning in 841 BC when he paid tribute to King Shalmaneser III.

- The *second* is the fact that the person who is paying tribute has a beard that is trimmed and the Law of Moses does not permit Israelites to trim their beards. This makes Dr Jones very sceptical that the person who is depicted as Jehu is, in fact, Jehu or even an Israelite. A cursory reading of the historical books of the Old Testament will quickly show that the Israelites did not keep the Law—that is why the Lord punished them over and over again and why they were eventually taken into captivity just as the Lord promised would happen to them.

- The *third* and final reason is that this tribute-paying is *not* mentioned in the Bible and so, Dr Jones dismisses it as being tribute from Israel, in spite of its being universally recognized by Assyrian academics and almost all Bible scholars as such. There are many instances of the kings of the Northern Kingdom of Israel paying tribute to the Assyrians that are recorded in the Assyrian Annals but are not recorded in the Bible. This does not mean that this tribute was not paid—it just means that it is not recorded in the Scriptures for one reason or another.

When these reasons are examined, we see that they are weak and can easily be dismissed and so, we can be absolutely sure that we are really seeing a carving of King Jehu on the Black Obelisk paying tribute to King Shalmaneser III of Assyria in 841 BC. It should also be noted that at the time of writing (AD 2021) this carving of King Jehu is the earliest known depiction of an Israelite king.

I now want to point out a further problem with the biblical chronology which is used by Dr Jones and many other American theologians, including the homeschoolers who accept this chronology. This concerns the reign of King Jehoash of the Northern Kingdom of Israel.

- According to the chronology that is used by Dr Jones and other American theologians,[7],[8] including the homeschoolers, King Jehoash reigned from 840 BC to 825 BC.
- According to Old Testament chronology, King Jehoahaz died in 798 BC and he was succeeded by his son Jehoash who then reigned for sixteen years from 798 BC to 782 BC.
- The Assyrian King, Adad-nirari III, reigned from 811 BC to 783 BC.
- Although not mentioned in the Scriptures, there is a

reference to King Jehoash paying tribute in 796 BC to the Assyrian King, Adad-nirari III, on a stela, which was found in 1967 at Tell al Rimah—about 50 miles (80 kilometres) west of Mosul in Iraq.

The above four, bullet-pointed paragraphs show that the biblical chronology, which is used by Dr Jones and other American theologians, including the homeschoolers, has King Jehoash dying fourteen years before the Assyrian King, Adad-nirari III, began to reign. This would make it totally impossible for King Jehoash to pay tribute in 796 BC to the Assyrian King because, according to their erroneous chronology, King Jehoash would have died twenty-nine years earlier in 825 BC. This shows that this chronology is not correct and that anyone who follows it and uses it should be aware of this.

NOTES

1 A J Monty White, *Rogues in Royal Robes*, (Leominster: Day One Publications, 2020).

2 Edwin R Thiele, *The Mysterious Numbers of the Hebrew Kings,* (Grand Rapids, MI: Kregel, 1983).

3 Many of these books are used by parents who homeschool their children in the USA and in the UK; and by teachers and pupils in schools in the USA that use books popular with so-called 'homeschoolers'.

4 James Ussher, *The Annals of the World,* (Green Forest, AR: Master Books, first published in 1658, revised & updated by Larry and Marion Pierce in 2003).

5 Floyd Nolen Jones, *The Chronology of the Old Testament* [4th Printing], (Green Forest, AR: Master Books, 2009), pp. 170–173.

6 Floyd Nolen Jones, *The Chronology of the Old Testament,* pp. 152–157.

7 B. Horton, [Editor], *Kings of Israel* [Student Study Outline, 3rd Edition], (Pensacola, Florida: A Beka Book, 2017), p. 251.

8 Floyd Nolen Jones, *The Chronology of the Old Testament,* pp.141 onwards.